Editors
Mary S. Jones, M.A.
Cristina Krysinski, M. Ed.

Editor in Chief
Karen J. Goldfluss, M.S. Ed.

Creative Director
Sarah M. Smith

Cover Artist
Diem Pascarella

Art Coordinator
Renée McElwee

Imaging
Ariyanna Simien

Publisher
Mary D. Smith, M.S. Ed.

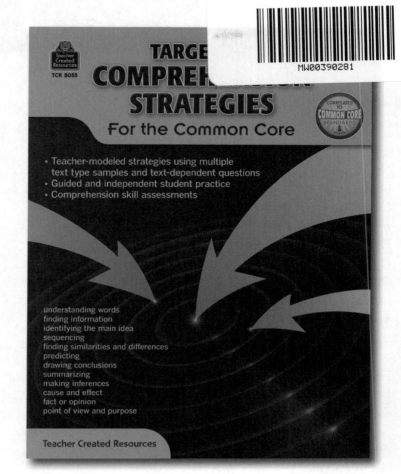

TCR 8055

TARGE COMPREHENSION STRATEGIES
For the Common Core

- Teacher-modeled strategies using multiple text type samples and text-dependent questions
- Guided and independent student practice
- Comprehension skill assessments

understanding words
finding information
identifying the main idea
sequencing
finding similarities and differences
predicting
drawing conclusions
summarizing
making inferences
cause and effect
fact or opinion
point of view and purpose

Teacher Created Resources

The lessons and activities in each unit have been correlated to Common Core State Standards for English Language Arts. Correlations charts are provided on pages 7 and 8 and can also be found at *http://www.teachercreated.com/standards*.

Teacher Created Resources
6421 Industry Way
Westminster, CA 92683
www.teachercreated.com
ISBN: 978-1-4206-8055-3
© 2014 Teacher Created Resources
Made in U.S.A.

Table of Contents

Introduction 3

About the Book and Lessons 4

Common Core State Standards Correlations 7

Unit 1

Lesson Notes and Activity Answers 9

Learning About the Strategies: Helpful Hints 12

Understanding Words: The Pyraminds 13

Understanding Words: The Beach 17

Finding Information: Crocodiles 19

Finding Information: Novus Bus Schedule 23

Identifying the Main Idea: Surfing 25

Identifying the Main Idea: A True Performer 29

Assessments: Mount Tambora 31

Unit 2

Lesson Notes and Activity Answers 35

Learning About the Strategies: Helpful Hints 38

Sequencing: Fun with the Dunns 39

Sequencing: Writing a Spy Novel 43

Finding Similarities and Differences: Leopards and Cheetahs . . 45

Finding Similarities and Differences: Bigfoot? 49

Predicting: Lost! 51

Predicting: Moonlight Forest 55

Assessments: Terrible Twins' Tale to Hit Big Screen 57

Unit 3

Lesson Notes and Activity Answers 61

Learning About the Strategies: Helpful Hints 64

Drawing Conclusions: The Mystery of *Mary Celeste* 65

Drawing Conclusions: The Castle Tour 69

Summarizing: Wolfgang Amadeus Mozart 71

Summarizing: Reality TV 75

Making Inferences: Ballet on a Board 77

Making Inferences: To Be Sold by Auction 81

Assessments: Aunty Belinda and Uncle Pete 83

Unit 4

Lesson Notes and Activity Answers 87

Learning About the Strategies: Helpful Hints 90

Cause and Effect: Easter Island 91

Cause and Effect: Exercise Is Good for You 95

Fact or Opinion: The Beauty of Slovenia 97

Fact or Opinion: Fabulous French Cuisine 101

Point of View and Purpose: Household Chores 103

Point of View and Purpose: The Wind in the Willows 107

Assessments: Stage Fright 109

What Is Comprehension?

Comprehension is a cognitive process. It involves the capacity of the mind to understand, using logic and reasoning. For students, it should be more than a process of trying to guess the answers to formal exercises after reading text. Students need to know **how to think about and make decisions about a text before, during, and after reading it**.

Teaching Comprehension

Comprehension skills can and should be developed by teaching students strategies that are appropriate to a particular comprehension skill and then providing opportunities for them to discuss and practice applying those strategies to the texts they read. These strategies can be a series of clearly defined steps to follow.

Students need to understand that it is the **process**—not the product—that is more important. In other words, they need to understand how it is done before they are required to demonstrate that they can do it.

Higher-order comprehension skills are within the capacity of young students, but care needs to be taken to ensure that the level and language of the text is appropriately assigned.

The text can be read to the students. When introducing comprehension strategies to students, the emphasis should be on the discussion, and the comprehension activities should be completed orally before moving on to supported and then independent practice and application. The lessons in this book are scaffolded to accommodate this process.

Note: Some students may not be able to complete the activities independently. For those students, additional support should be provided as they work through the activities within each unit.

Before students start the activities in this book, discuss the concepts of paragraphs and stanzas. Note that the paragraphs in each reading passage or stanza have been numbered for easy reference as students complete activities.

The terms *skills* and *strategies* are sometimes confused. The following explanation provides some clarification of how the two terms are used in this book.

Skills relate to competent performance and come from knowledge, practice, and aptitude.

Strategies involve planning and tactics.

In other words, we can teach *strategies* that will help students acquire specific comprehension *skills*.

Twelve comprehension skills are introduced in this book. Information about these skills and how the units and lessons are designed to explore them are provided on pages 4 – 6.

Metacognitive Strategies

Metacognitive strategies, which involve teaching students how to think about thinking, are utilized in developing the twelve comprehension skills taught in this book. Metacognitive strategies are modeled and explained to students for each skill. As this is essentially an oral process, teachers are encouraged to elaborate on and discuss the explanations provided on each "Learning Page." The activities on these pages allow students to talk about the different thought processes they would use in answering each question.

Students will require different levels of support before they are able to work independently to comprehend, make decisions about text, and choose the best answer in multiple-choice questions. This support is provided within each unit lesson by including guided practice, modeled practice using the metacognitive processes, and assisted practice using hints and clues.

Comprehension Strategies

The exercises in this book have been written—not to test—but to stimulate and challenge students and to help them develop their thinking processes through modeled metacognitive strategies, discussion, and guided and independent practice. There are no trick questions, but many require and encourage students to use logic and reasoning.

Particularly in the higher-order comprehension skills, there may be more than one acceptable answer. The reader's prior knowledge and experience will influence some of his or her decisions about the text. Teachers may choose to accept an answer if a student can justify and explain his or her choice. Therefore, some of the answers provided should not be considered prescriptive but more of a guide and a basis for discussion.

Some students with excellent cognitive processing skills, who have a particular aptitude for and acquire an interest in reading, tend to develop advanced reading comprehension skills independently. However, for the majority of students, the strategies they need to develop and demonstrate comprehension need to be made explicit and carefully guided, not just tested, which is the rationale behind this series of books.

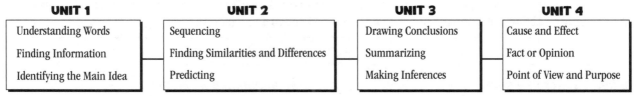

About the Book and Lessons

The following twelve comprehension skills are included in this book. Strategies for improving these skills are provided through sets of lessons for each of the skills. These twelve skills have been divided into four units, each with teachers' notes and answer keys, three different comprehension skills, and three student assessment tests.

UNIT 1

Understanding Words

Finding Information

Identifying the Main Idea

UNIT 2

Sequencing

Finding Similarities and Differences

Predicting

UNIT 3

Drawing Conclusions

Summarizing

Making Inferences

UNIT 4

Cause and Effect

Fact or Opinion

Point of View and Purpose

Each skill listed above has a six-page lesson to help students build stronger comprehension skills in that area by using specific strategies.

- Text 1 (first reading text page for use with practice pages)
- Learning Page (learning about the skill with teacher modeling)
- Practice Page (student practice with teacher assistance)
- On Your Own (independent student activity)
- Text 2 (second reading text page for use with practice page)
- Try It Out (independent student activity with one clue)

A test at the end of each unit assesses the three skills taught in the unit. The assessment section includes:

- Assessment Text (reading text used for all three assessments)
- Assessment test for the first skill in the unit
- Assessment test for the second skill in the unit
- Assessment test for the third skill in the unit

 Included in this book is a CD containing reproducible, PDF-formatted files for all activity pages, as well as Common Core State Standards. The PDF files are ideal for group instruction using interactive whiteboards.

Text Types

In addition to applying comprehension strategies to better understand content, students will experience reading and interpreting a variety of text types:

- Reports
- Narratives
- Expositions
- Recounts
- Procedures
- Explanations

Teacher and Student Pages

Lesson Notes

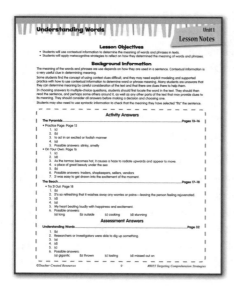

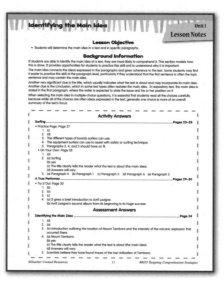

Each of the four units contains lessons that address three specific comprehension skills. Every Lesson Notes page includes:

- Lesson objective indicators state expected outcomes.

- Background information about the skill and teaching strategies.

- An answer key for student pages and assessment pages. (*Note:* Answers may vary, particularly with higher-order comprehension skills. Teachers may choose to accept alternative answers if students are able to justify their responses.)

Helpful Hints

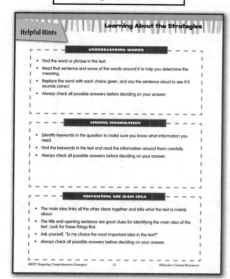

- All three comprehension skills for the unit are identified. These serve as reminders for students as they complete the activities.

- Helpful hints are provided for each skill in bullet-point form.

Text 1

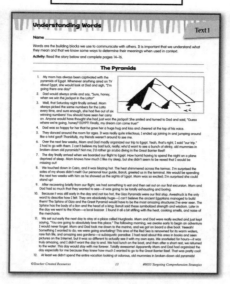

- The skill is identified and defined.

- The text is presented to students using oral, silent, partner, or read-aloud methods. Choose a technique or approach most suitable to your classroom needs.

Learning Page

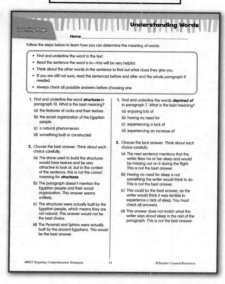

- This is a teacher-student interaction page.

- Steps and strategies are outlined, discussed, and referenced using the text page.

- Multiple-choice questions are presented, and metacognitive processes for choosing the best answer are described.

Practice Page

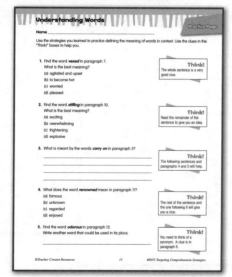

- Using the text page content, students practice strategies to complete the questions. The teacher provides guidance as needed.

- Some multiple-choice questions and others requiring explanations are presented with prompts or clues to assist students.

On Your Own

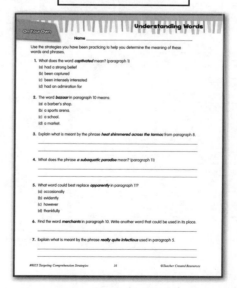

- This page is completed independently.

- At least one multiple-choice question and others requiring explanations are presented for students to complete.

Text 2

- As with the first text page for the lesson, the skill is identified.

- Presentation of the text is decided by the teacher.

Try It Out

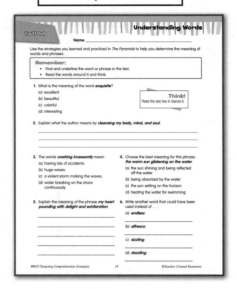

- This page can be completed independently by the student.

- Multiple-choice questions and some requiring explanation are included.

Assessment Text

- The three skills to be tested are identified.

- The assessment text is presented.

Unit Assessments

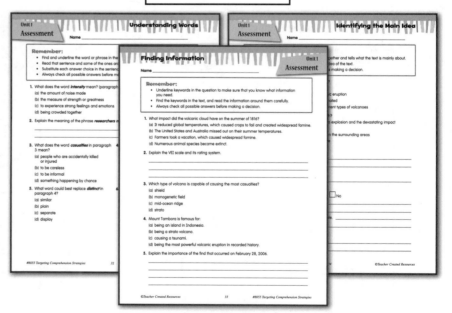

- An assessment page is provided for each of the three skills in the unit.

- The comprehension skill to be tested is identified, and students apply their knowledge and strategies to complete each page, using the content of the Assessment Text page.

- Multiple-choice questions and others requiring more explanation are presented.

Each lesson meets one or more of the following Common Core State Standards © Copyright 2010. National Governors Association Center for Best Practices and Council of Chief State School Officers. All rights reserved. For more information about the Common Core State Standards, go to *http://www.corestandards.org/* or *http://www.teachercreated.com/standards*.

READING: LITERATURE STANDARDS	Pages
Key Ideas and Details	
ELA.RL.8.1: Cite the textual evidence that most strongly supports an analysis of what the text says explicitly as well as inferences drawn from the text.	39-42, 49-50, 51-54, 55-56, 69-70, 77-80, 81-82, 83-86, 103-106, 109-112
ELA.RL.8.2: Determine a theme or central idea of a text and analyze its development over the course of the text, including its relationship to the characters, setting, and plot; provide an objective summary of the text.	39-42, 43-44, 51-54, 55-56, 69-70, 75-76, 77-80, 81-82, 83-86, 109-112
ELA.RL.8.3: Analyze how particular lines of dialogue or incidents in a story or drama propel the action, reveal aspects of a character, or provoke a decision.	17-18, 39-42, 51-54, 69-70, 75-76, 77-80, 81-82, 83-86, 103-106, 109-112
Craft and Structure	
ELA.RL.8.4: Determine the meaning of words and phrases as they are used in a text, including figurative and connotative meanings; analyze the impact of specific word choices on meaning and tone, including analogies or allusions to other texts.	17-18, 39-42, 43-44, 49-50, 51-54, 55-56, 69-70, 75-76, 77-80, 81-82, 83-86, 103-106, 109-112
ELA.RL.8.6: Analyze how differences in the points of view of the characters and the audience or reader (e.g., created through the use of dramatic irony) create such effects as suspense or humor.	39-42, 49-50, 51-54, 69-70, 75-76, 83-86, 103-106, 109-112
Range of Reading and Level of Text Complexity	
ELA.RL.8.10: By the end of the year, read and comprehend literature, including stories, dramas, and poems, at the high end of grades 6–8 text complexity band independently and proficiently.	All passages allow students to read and comprehend literature at the high end of the grades 6–8 text complexity band.

READING: INFORMATIONAL TEXT STANDARDS	Pages
Key Ideas and Details	
ELA.RI.8.1: Cite the textual evidence that most strongly supports an analysis of what the text says explicitly as well as inferences drawn from the text.	19-22, 23-24, 25-28, 29-30, 31-34, 45-48, 57-60, 65-68, 71-74, 91-94, 97-100, 101-102
ELA.RI.8.2: Determine a central idea of a text and analyze its development over the course of the text, including its relationship to supporting ideas; provide an objective summary of the text.	13-16, 19-22, 25-28, 29-30, 31-34, 45-48, 57-60, 65-68, 71-74, 91-94, 95-96, 97-100, 101-102
ELA.RI.8.3: Analyze how a text makes connections among and distinctions between individuals, ideas, or events (e.g., through comparisons, analogies, or categories).	19-22, 23-24, 25-28, 31-34, 45-48, 57-60, 65-68, 71-74, 91-94, 95-96, 97-100, 101-102, 107-108
Craft and Structure	
ELA.RI.8.4: Determine the meaning of words and phrases as they are used in a text, including figurative, connotative, and technical meanings; analyze the impact of specific word choices on meaning and tone, including analogies or allusions to other texts.	13-16, 19-22, 23-24, 25-28, 29-30, 31-34, 45-48, 57-60, 65-68, 71-74, 91-94, 95-96, 97-100, 101-102, 107-108
ELA.RI.8.5: Analyze in detail the structure of a specific paragraph in a text, including the role of particular sentences in developing and refining a key concept.	13-16, 19-22, 25-28, 29-30, 31-34, 65-68, 71-74, 91-94, 95-96, 97-100, 101-102
ELA.RI.8.6: Determine an author's point of view or purpose in a text and analyze how the author acknowledges and responds to conflicting evidence or viewpoints.	97-100, 101-102, 107-108
Range of Reading and Level of Text Complexity	
ELA.RI.8.10: By the end of the year, read and comprehend literary nonfiction at the high end of the grades 6–8 text complexity band independently and proficiently.	All passages allow students to read and comprehend literary nonfiction at the high end of the grades 6–8 text complexity band.

Lesson Objectives

- Students will use contextual information to determine the meaning of words and phrases in texts.
- Students will apply metacognitive strategies to reflect on how they determined the meaning of words and phrases.

Background Information

The meaning of the words and phrases we use depends on how they are used in a sentence. Contextual information is a very useful clue in determining meaning.

Some students find the concept of using context clues difficult, and they may need explicit modeling and supported practice with how to use contextual information to determine word or phrase meaning. Many students are unaware that they can determine meaning by careful consideration of the text and that there are clues there to help them.

In choosing answers to multiple-choice questions, students should first locate the word in the text. They should then read the sentence, and perhaps some others around it, as well as any other parts of the text that may provide clues to its meaning. They should consider all answers before making a decision and choosing one.

Students may also need to use syntactic information to check that the meaning they have selected "fits" the sentence.

Activity Answers

The Pyramids..**Pages 13–16**

- Practice Page: Page 15
    1. (c)
    2. (b)
    3. to act in an excited or foolish manner
    4. (a)
    5. Possible answers: stinky, smelly
- On Your Own: Page 16
    1. (c)
    2. (d)
    3. As the tarmac becomes hot, it causes a haze to radiate upwards and appear to move.
    4. a place of great beauty under the sea
    5. (b)
    6. Possible answers: traders, shopkeepers, sellers, vendors
    7. It was easy to get drawn into the excitement of the moment.

The Beach..**Pages 17–18**

- Try It Out: Page 18
    1. (b)
    2. It's so refreshing that it washes away any worries or pains—leaving the person feeling rejuvenated.
    3. (d)
    4. (a)
    5. My heart beating loudly with happiness and excitement.
    6. Possible answers:
        (a) long   (b) outside   (c) cooking   (d) stunning

Assessment Answers

Understanding Words..**Page 32**

    1. (b)
    2. Researchers or investigators were able to dig up something.
    3. (a)
    4. (d)
    5. (c)
    6. Possible answers:
        (a) gigantic   (b) thrown   (c) lasting   (d) missed out on

Lesson Notes

Lesson Objectives

- Students will scan text to locate keywords.
- Students will read text carefully, as many times as necessary, to find important and supporting information and details.

Background Information

This section models and explains how to locate keywords in questions and then in the text. Students are encouraged to scan a text to identify keywords and reread the text a number of times, if necessary, to locate details. They should then be able to determine which details are important in clarifying information and in supporting their ideas and the choices they have made.

Many students are unaware of the need to return to the text, or even that this is permitted, and believe they should have understood and remembered all details from their first reading.

Having identified the keyword in a question, some students find it difficult to scan the text to locate these words. It is suggested that they are assisted by being given additional information; for example, the specific paragraph they need to read. Many may not be aware that the first sentence in a paragraph often tells what that particular paragraph is about, and reading it quickly can be very helpful.

When locating details in informational text, particular care should be taken to ensure that the information is accurate and that it is recorded correctly. Although there is generally more room for interpretation in fiction, this skill requires students to locate information that is stated in the text.

Activity Answers

Crocodiles...**Pages 19–22**

- Practice Page: Page 21
    1. crocodiles, alligators, caimans
    2. jaws, teeth, tail
    3. (a) fish, frogs, snakes, turtles, waterbirds, and other small animals
       (b) fish, crabs, insects, turtles, birds, other reptiles, dingoes, wallabies, cattle, horses, and people
    4. (d)
    5. Its voracious appetite—it basically ran out of food to eat!
- On Your Own: Page 22
    1. It gave scientists the direct ancestor to the modern-day crocodiles.
    2. (a) *Crocodylus porosus*   (b) *Crocodylus johnstoni*
    3. (b)
    4. It waits, hidden near the water's edge. It then propels itself at high speed out of the water using its tail. It then grabs its prey and drags it into the water, drowning the victim.
    5. (a) 2,200; 68   (b) 17,500; 132   (c) 1970   (d) 10; 6.5   (e) 23

Novus Bus Schedule ....**Pages 23–24**

- Try It Out: Page 24
    1. (a) 8:37 a.m.   (b) 10:17 p.m.   (c) 12:05 p.m.   (d) 6:43 a.m.
    2. Novus City   3. 883, 884   4. 53 minutes   5. three times
    6. Monday, Tuesday, Wednesday, Thursday, Friday (weekdays)
    7. 10:37 a.m.   8. 5:18 p.m.   9. 11:54 a.m.   10. 10:07 a.m.

Assessment Answers

Finding Information ....**Page 33**

1. (a)
2. It is used to measure the intensity of a volcano. It rates 0–8, 0 being non-explosive and 8 being mega-colossal.
3. (d)
4. (d)
5. Artifacts from the village at Mount Tambora give us a glimpse into what life was like for the Indonesian people at that time.

Lesson Objective

- Students will determine the main idea in a text and in specific paragraphs.

Background Information

If students are able to identify the main idea of a text, they are more likely to comprehend it. This section models how this is done. It provides opportunities for students to practice this skill and to understand why it is important.

The main idea connects the ideas expressed in the paragraphs and gives coherence to the text. Some students may find it easier to practice this skill at the paragraph level, particularly if they understand that the first sentence is often the topic sentence and may contain the main idea.

Another very significant clue is the title, which usually indicates what the text is about and may incorporate its main idea. Another clue is the conclusion, which in some text types often restates the main idea. In expository text, the main idea is stated in the first paragraph, where the writer is expected to state the issue and his or her position on it.

When selecting the main idea in multiple-choice questions, it is essential that students read all the choices carefully, because while all of the choices are often ideas expressed in the text, generally one choice is more of an overall summary of the text's focus.

Activity Answers

Surfing .... **Pages 25–28**

- Practice Page: Page 27
    1. (c)
    2. (d)
    3. The different types of boards surfers can use.
    4. The equipment surfers can use to assist with safety or surfing technique.
    5. Paragraphs 3, 4, and 5 should have an **X**.
- On Your Own: Page 28
    1. (a)
    2. (a) Surfing
       (b) yes
       (c) The title clearly tells the reader what the text is about (the main idea).
       (d) Answers will vary.
    3. (a) Paragraph 4   (b) Paragraph 1   (c) Paragraph 3   (d) Paragraph 6   (e) Paragraph 5

A True Performer .... **Pages 29–30**

- Try It Out: Page 30
    1. (b)
    2. (a)
    3. (c)
    4. (a) It gives a brief introduction to Avril Lavigne.
       (b) Avril Lavigne's second album from its beginning to its huge success

Assessment Answers

Identifying the Main Idea .... **Page 34**

    1. (d)
    2. (a)
    3. An introduction outlining the location of Mount Tambora and the intensity of the volcanic explosion that occurred there
    4. (a) Mount Tambora
       (b) yes
       (c) The title clearly tells the reader what the text is about (the main idea).
       (d) Answers will vary.
    5. Scientists believe they have found traces of the lost civilization of Tambora.

UNDERSTANDING WORDS

- Find the word or phrase in the text.

- Read that sentence and some of the words around it to help you determine the meaning.

- Replace the word with each choice given, and say the sentence aloud to see if it sounds correct.

- Always check all possible answers before deciding on your answer.

FINDING INFORMATION

- Identify keywords in the question to make sure you know what information you need.

- Find the keywords in the text and read the information around them carefully.

- Always check all possible answers before deciding on your answer.

IDENTIFYING THE MAIN IDEA

- The main idea links all the other ideas together and tells what the text is mainly about.

- The title and opening sentence are good clues for identifying the main idea of the text. Look for these things first.

- Ask yourself, "Is my choice the most important idea in the text?"

- Always check all possible answers before deciding on your answer.

Understanding Words

Name _____

Words are the building blocks we use to communicate with others. It is important that we understand what they mean and that we know some ways to determine their meanings when used in context.

Activity: Read the story below and complete pages 14–16.

The Pyramids

1. My mom has always been captivated with the pyramids of Egypt. Whenever anything aired on TV about Egypt, she would look at Dad and sigh, "I'm going there one day!"

2. Dad would always smile and say, "Sure, honey, when we win the jackpot in the Lotto!"

3. Well, that Saturday night finally arrived. Mom always picked the same numbers for the Lotto every time, and sure enough, she had five out of six winning numbers! You should have seen her carry on. Anyone would have thought she had just won the jackpot! She smiled and turned to Dad and said, "Guess where we're going, honey? EGYPT! Finally, my dream can come true!"

4. Dad was so happy for her that he gave her a huge hug and kiss and cheered at the top of his voice.

5. They danced around the room for ages. It was really quite infectious; I ended up joining in and jumping around like a total goof! Thankfully, my friends weren't around to see me.

6. Over the next few weeks, Mom and Dad madly organized our trip to Egypt. Yeah, that's right, I said "our trip." I had to go with them. I can't believe my bad luck, really; who'd want to see a bunch of stinky, old mummies in broken-down old pyramids? Not me; I'd rather go scuba diving in the Great Barrier Reef!

7. The day finally arrived when we boarded our flight to Egypt. How horrid having to spend the night on a plane deprived of sleep. Mom knows how much I like my sleep, but she didn't seem to be vexed that I would be missing out!

8. We touched down in Cairo, and it was blazing hot. The heat shimmered across the tarmac. I'm surprised the soles of my shoes didn't melt! Our personal tour guide, Baruti, greeted us in the terminal. We would be spending the next two weeks with him as he showed us the sights of Egypt. Mom was so excited; I'm surprised she could stand up!

9. After recovering briefly from our flight, we had something to eat and then set out on our first excursion. Mom and Dad had so much that they wanted to see—it was going to be totally exhausting and boring.

10. Because it was still early in the day and not too hot, the Giza Pyramids were our first stop. Awestruck is the only word to describe how I felt. They are absolutely huge—I can't believe the ancient Egyptians managed to build them! The Sphinx of Giza and the Great Pyramid would have to be the most amazing structures I've ever seen. The Sphinx has the body of a lion and the head of a king; Baruti said these symbolized strength and wisdom. Later in the day we went to the Khan—a local bazaar. I found it all a bit stifling with the heat, cooking smells, and noise of the merchants.

11. We set out early the next day to stay at a place called Hurghada. Mom and Dad were really excited and just kept saying, "You are going to absolutely love this place." The following morning, we awoke early to begin an adventure I would never forget. Mom and Dad took me down to the marina, and we got on board a dive boat. Yeeeah! Something I wanted to do; we were going snorkeling! This area of the Red Sea is renowned for its warm waters, rare fish life, and amazing sea gardens—a subaquatic paradise. I had read about this area in books and seen pictures on the Internet, but it was so different to actually see it with my own eyes. We snorkeled for hours—it was truly amazing, and I didn't want the day to end. We had lunch on the boat, and then after a short rest, we returned to the water. This day would stay with me forever. Totally awesome! Apparently Mom and Dad had organized the day especially for me because they knew how much I wanted to go to the Great Barrier Reef. That was pretty cool!

12. At least we didn't spend the entire vacation looking at odorous, old mummies in broken-down old pyramids!

Name _____

Follow the steps below to learn how you can determine the meaning of words.

- Find and underline the word in the text.
- Read the sentence the word is in—this will be very helpful.
- Think about the other words in the sentence to find out what clues they give you.
- If you are still not sure, read the sentences before and after and the whole paragraph if needed.
- Always check all possible answers before choosing one.

1. Find and underline the word **structures** in paragraph 10. What is the best meaning?

    (a) the features of rocks and their texture

    (b) the social organization of the Egyptian people

    (c) a natural phenomenon

    (d) something built or constructed

2. Choose the best answer. Think about each choice carefully.

    (a) The stone used to build the structures would have texture and be very attractive to look at, but in the context of the sentence, this is not the correct meaning for **structures**.

    (b) The paragraph doesn't mention the Egyptian people and their social organization. This answer seems unlikely.

    (c) The structures were actually built by the Egyptian people, which means they are not natural. This answer would not be the best choice.

    (d) The Pyramid and Sphinx were actually built by the ancient Egyptians. This would be the best answer.

1. Find and underline the words **deprived of** in paragraph 7. What is the best meaning?

    (a) enjoying lots of

    (b) having no need for

    (c) experiencing a lack of

    (d) experiencing an increase of

2. Choose the best answer. Think about each choice carefully.

    (a) The next sentence mentions that the writer likes his or her sleep and would be missing out on it during the flight. This is not the best answer.

    (b) Having no need for sleep is not something the writer would think to do. This is not the best answer.

    (c) This could be the best answer, as the writer would think it was terrible to experience a lack of sleep. You must check all answers.

    (d) This answer does not match what the writer says about sleep in the rest of the paragraph. This is not the best answer.

Understanding Words

Name _____

Use the strategies you learned to practice defining the meaning of words in context. Use the clues in the "Think!" boxes to help you.

1. Find the word **vexed** in paragraph 7.
   What is the best meaning?
   (a) agitated and upset
   (b) to become hot
   (c) worried
   (d) pleased

   Think!
   The whole sentence is a very good clue.

2. Find the word **stifling** in paragraph 10.
   What is the best meaning?
   (a) exciting
   (b) overwhelming
   (c) frightening
   (d) explosive

   Think!
   Read the remainder of the sentence to give you an idea.

3. What is meant by the words **carry on** in paragraph 3?

   _____
   _____
   _____
   _____

   Think!
   The following sentences and paragraphs 4 and 5 will help.

4. What does the word **renowned** mean in paragraph 11?
   (a) famous
   (b) unknown
   (c) regarded
   (d) enjoyed

   Think!
   The rest of the sentence and the one following it will give you a clue.

5. Find the word **odorous** in paragraph 12.
   Write another word that could be used in its place.

   _____

   Think!
   You need to think of a synonym. A clue is in paragraph 6.

Name _____

Use the strategies you have been practicing to help you determine the meaning of these words and phrases.

1. What does the word **captivated** mean? (paragraph 1)
   (a) had a strong belief
   (b) been captured
   (c) been intensely interested
   (d) had an admiration for

2. The word **bazaar** in paragraph 10 means:
   (a) a barber's shop.
   (b) a sports arena.
   (c) a school.
   (d) a market.

3. Explain what is meant by the phrase **heat shimmered across the tarmac** from paragraph 8.

   _____

   _____

4. What does the phrase **a subaquatic paradise** mean? (paragraph 11)

   _____

   _____

5. What word could best replace **apparently** in paragraph 11?
   (a) occasionally
   (b) evidently
   (c) however
   (d) thankfully

6. Find the word **merchants** in paragraph 10. Write another word that could be used in its place.

   _____

7. Explain what is meant by the phrase **really quite infectious** used in paragraph 5.

   _____

   _____

Understanding Words

Name _____

Activity: Read the poem below and complete page 18.

The Beach

1. Oooh, I love the beach
   the soft white sand beneath my bare feet
   shifting with my movements
   oozing between my hot, smelly toes.

2. Oooh, I love the beach
   the freedom of frolicking in the ocean
   the cool water washing over me
   cleansing my body, mind, and soul.

3. Oooh, I love the beach
   the warm sun glistening on the water
   the gentle breeze blowing over me
   calming me, cooling me, relaxing me.

4. Oooh, I love the beach
   breathing the clean air into my lungs
   walking, splashing along the water's edge
   every part of my body feeling alive and glowing.

5. Oooh, I love the beach
   seeing the dolphins playing in the sea
   breaching, jumping, chasing, and rolling
   my heart pounding with delight and exhilaration.

6. Oooh, I love the beach
   endless summers surfing and swimming
   snorkeling through the exquisite reef
   the awesome might of nature there for all to see.

7. Oooh, I love the beach
   the waves crashing incessantly
   always moving, always living, never stopping
   demonstrating the power they have over me.

8. Oooh, I love the beach
   icy ice pops dripping down my arm
   hot dogs sizzling on the barbeque
   eating alfresco under the bright twinkling stars.

9. Oooh, I love the beach
   the bright colors of the umbrellas, towels, and swimsuits
   red, yellow, orange, and blue
   like a dazzling rainbow filling up my senses.

10. Oooh, I love the beach!

Try It Out

Name _____

Use the strategies you learned and practiced in *The Pyramids* to help you determine the meaning of words and phrases.

Remember:
- Find and underline the word or phrase in the text.
- Read the words around it and think.

---

1. What is the meaning of the word **exquisite**?

   (a) excellent

   (b) beautiful

   (c) colorful

   (d) interesting

   Think!
   Read the last line in stanza 6.

2. Explain what the author means by **cleansing my body, mind, and soul**.

   _____

   _____

   _____

3. The words **crashing incessantly** mean:

   (a) having lots of accidents.

   (b) huge waves.

   (c) a violent storm making the waves.

   (d) water breaking on the shore continuously.

4. Choose the best meaning for this phrase: **the warm sun glistening on the water**.

   (a) the sun shining and being reflected off the water

   (b) being absorbed by the water

   (c) the sun setting on the horizon

   (d) heating the water for swimming

5. Explain the meaning of the phrase **my heart pounding with delight and exhilaration**.

   _____

   _____

   _____

   _____

6. Write another word that could have been used instead of . . .

   (a) **endless**:

   _____

   (b) **alfresco**:

   _____

   (c) **sizzling**:

   _____

   (d) **dazzling**:

   _____

Name _____

When you read text, you can usually remember some of the information. If you are asked about details, you should refer back to the text to locate and check that the information is correct. Remember, the answer you are looking for is there in the text—you just need to find it.

Activity: Read the passage below and complete pages 20–22.

Crocodiles

1. Crocodile-like reptiles existed before dinosaurs about 230 million years ago (mya). These remarkably adaptable creatures outlasted the mass extinction of the dinosaurs to evolve into the 23 species of crocodilians around today. *Crocodilian* is the name given to the group of reptiles that includes crocodiles, alligators, and caimans. They have changed very little over the last 65 million years.

2. One prehistoric species was the *Sarchosuchus imperator* (flesh crocodile emperor), also known as "super-croc." It was discovered in Niger in Africa and lived about 110 mya. It grew to a length of around 35 feet (dwarfing the crocodilians of today) and weighed in at a hefty 17,500 pounds; the skull alone measured 6.5 feet in length and held 132 teeth. This carnivore had a voracious appetite and probably died out as a result of this. It is not a direct relative of the crocodile of today but is a very impressive close cousin. The link between the ancient and the modern crocodile was finally discovered in Isisford, a small town in central-western Queensland, Australia. The discovery of *Isisfordia duncani* in the mid-1990s gave scientists the direct ancestor to modern-day crocodiles. This crocodile lived about 98–95 mya, grew to over 3 feet in length, and weighed in at around 6½ pounds—relatively small in comparison to the crocodiles of today.

3. Crocodiles are a formidable reptile considered to be at the top of the food chain. They are believed to be highly intelligent animals that have been known to hunt and stalk their prey. Crocodiles are able to last long periods between feeding—probably contributing to the success of the species. The continent of Australia is home to two species of the modern crocodile: the freshwater crocodile (*Crocodylus johnstoni*) and the saltwater or estuarine crocodile (*Crocodylus porosus*).

4. The freshwater crocodile is found in Northern Australia and lives in freshwater rivers, gorges, and billabongs. The freshwater crocodile is smaller than its saltwater counterpart, with males growing to about 10 feet long and females to about 6½ feet. This species of crocodile is not considered dangerous to humans, as its diet generally consists of fish, frogs, snakes, turtles, waterbirds, and other small animals. It mainly hunts at night and rests and recuperates during the day. The freshwater crocodile has a long, smooth, slender snout, as opposed to the saltwater crocodile, which has a shorter, wider snout.

5. The saltwater crocodile is the largest species of crocodile, with males growing up to 23 feet in length and weighing in at around 2,200 pounds, while the females can grow to a length of about 13 feet. The saltwater crocodile can be found along estuaries, rivers, lagoons, swamps, and beaches in Southeast Asia and Northern Australia. The stealthy crocodile waits near the water's edge, pounces out of the water at its unsuspecting prey, then drags it under the water. The prey is usually stored underwater for several days to soften before the crocodile returns for its meal. The saltwater crocodile dines on a variety of foods from fish, crabs, and insects to turtles, birds, other reptiles, dingoes, wallabies, cattle, horses, and occasionally people who do not follow safety precautions. Because of this, saltwater crocodiles were hunted almost to extinction in Australia until they became a protected species in 1970. Since then, numbers have increased.

6. One has to marvel at the power of the saltwater crocodile; its body was built to prey. The jaws deliver an incredible impact, and the 68 teeth are designed to hold prey, penetrate the skin, and crush the victim. The tail propels the crocodile over 30 feet out of the water at speeds faster than a racehorse, and it can administer a huge blow, easily breaking the legs of its victim to prevent an escape!

Learning Page

Name _____

Follow the steps below to learn how to find information in text.

- Underline the keywords in the question to make sure you know what information is needed.
- Find and underline the keywords in the text, and read the information around them carefully.
- Always check all possible answers before making a decision.

1. Crocodiles are:

(a) herbivores, eating only plants.

(b) omnivores, eating meat and plants.

(c) cannibals, eating each other.

(d) carnivores, eating only meat.

2. Choose the best answer. Think about each choice carefully.

(a) Crocodiles eat fish, frogs, snakes, turtles, waterbirds, small animals, and larger animals. No plants are mentioned, so this wouldn't be the best answer.

(b) There is no mention of crocodiles eating meat and plants. This answer seems unlikely.

(c) Nowhere in the text does it talk about crocodiles eating other crocodiles. This answer is not likely.

(d) The text clearly lists the food crocodiles generally eat. The entire list is made up of animals, which means crocodiles are carnivores. This would be the best answer.

1. Which species of crocodile is the largest living reptile in the world?

(a) *Sarchosuchus imperator*

(b) *Crocodylus porosus*

(c) *Crocodylus johnstoni*

(d) *Isisfordia duncani*

2. Choose the best answer. Think about each choice carefully.

(a) *Sarchosuchus imperator* was definitely large, probably the largest crocodile to ever roam Earth, but it isn't living. This is not the best answer.

(b) *Crocodylus porosus* is the proper name for the saltwater crocodile, which is the largest species of crocodile in the world today. It is also a reptile, so this would make it the largest living reptile in the world. This would be the best answer.

(c) *Crocodylus johnstoni* is the freshwater crocodile, which is smaller than the saltwater crocodile, so it can't be the largest. This wouldn't be a good choice.

(d) *Isisfordia duncani* is now extinct, so it's not living and was also smaller than the crocodiles of today. This wouldn't be a suitable answer.

Name _____

Use the strategies you learned to practice finding information. Use the clues in the "Think!" boxes to help you.

1. List the reptiles that belong in the *Crocodilian* family.

   _____

   _____

   Think!
   This information is in the first paragraph.

2. What features make the saltwater crocodile so formidable?

   _____

   _____

   Think!
   Read paragraph 6, and consider the parts of the crocodile that are strong and powerful.

3. Complete the sentences using words from the text.

   (a) A freshwater crocodile's diet consists of . . .

   _____

   _____

   _____

   (b) A saltwater crocodile's diet consists of . . .

   _____

   _____

   _____

   Think!
   Read paragraphs 4 and 5 to find the information needed.

4. Which species of crocodile is the direct ancestor of modern-day crocodiles?

   (a) *Crocodylus johnstoni*

   (b) *Crocodylus porosus*

   (c) *Sarchosuchus imperator*

   (d) *Isisfordia duncani*

   Think!
   Read paragraph 2.

5. What is considered to be the main cause of the extinction of the "super-croc"?

   _____

   _____

   _____

   _____

   Think!
   Consider the huge size of the species.

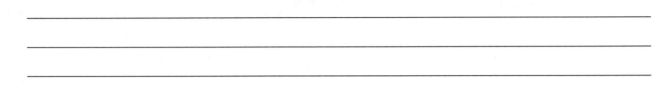

On Your Own

Name _____

Use the strategies you have been practicing to help you find information in the text.

1. Explain the importance of the discovery at Isisford.

   _____

   _____

   _____

   _____

2. Look at the pictures of the two crocodiles below. Match them to their correct name.

   (a)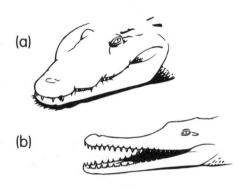

   (b)

   • *Crocodylus johnstoni*

   • *Crocodylus porosus*

3. Prehistoric *Sarchosuchus imperator* was discovered in:

   (a) Southeast Asia.   (b) Africa.

   (c) Northern Australia.   (d) America.

4. In your own words, explain how a saltwater crocodile catches and kills its prey.

   _____

   _____

   _____

   _____

5. Complete these number facts using figures from the text.

   (a) A male saltwater crocodile weighs around _____ pounds and has _____ teeth.

   (b) *Sarchosuchus imperator* weighed _____ pounds and had _____ teeth.

   (c) In Australia, saltwater crocodiles became a protected species in _____.

   (d) Male freshwater crocodiles grow to _____ feet and females to _____ feet.

   (e) At the present time, _____ species of crocodilians exist.

Finding Information

Name _____

Activity: Read the bus schedule below and complete page 24.

Novus Bus Schedule

TO NOVUS CITY					883, 884
Weekday Schedule					– no stop
Route No.	Targa Train Station	Tidas Road/ Gull Street	Tableworth Shopping Center	Creekville Shopping Center	City Busport
883 a.m.	–	6:28	6:43	6:57	7:12
884	–	6:52	7:02	7:17	7:32
883	–	7:01	7:17	7:32	7:47
884	–	7:16	–	7:42	7:57
883	–	7:17	7:32	–	–
883	–	7:26	7:42	7:57	8:12
884	–	7:47	7:57	8:12	8:27
883	–	8:21	8:37	8:51	9:05
884	8:37	8:54	9:08	9:21	9:35
883	9:07	9:24	9:38	9:51	10:05
884	9:37	9:54	10:08	10:21	10:35
883	10:07	10:24	10:38	10:51	11:05
884	10:37	10:54	11:08	11:21	11:35
883	11:07	11:24	–	11:51	12:05
884	11:37	11:54	12:08	12:21	12:35
883 p.m.	12:07	12:24	12:38	12:51	1:05
884	12:37	12:54	1:08	1:21	1:35
883	1:07	1:24	1:38	1:51	2:05
884	1:37	1:54	2:08	2:21	2:35
883	2:07	–	2:38	2:51	3:13
884	2:37	2:56	3:10	3:24	3:43
883	3:06	3:23	3:38	3:53	4:13
884	3:36	3:53	4:08	4:21	4:38
884	4:05	4:22	–	4:49	5:06
884	4:45	–	5:16	5:29	5:46
884	5:18	5:35	5:49	6:01	6:17
884	–	6:04	6:18	6:31	6:47
883	–	6:36	6:50	7:02	–
883	7:24	7:36	7:50	8:02	8:17
883	8:24	8:36	8:50	9:02	9:17
883	9:24	9:36	9:50	10:02	10:17

Name _____

Use the strategies you learned and practiced in *Crocodiles* to help you find information and details.

> ## Remember:
> - Determine the keywords and find them in the text.
> - Check all answers before you make a decision.

1. What time:

   (a) is the first bus to leave Targa Train Station? _____

   (b) does the bus service finish for the day? _____

   (c) is the first afternoon bus arrival at the City Busport? _____

   (d) is the earliest arrival at Tableworth Shopping Center?_____

2. In which city is the City Busport located? _____

3. Which two bus routes are listed on this timetable?

   _____

   _____

4. What is the total time it takes for the final bus of the day to make the journey from Targa Train Station to the City Busport?

   _____

5. How many times in the day does a bus pass by Tableworth Shopping Center without stopping?

   _____

6. Name the days of the week included in this bus schedule.

   _____

   _____

   _____

7. If I wanted to arrive at the City Busport right before 12:00 p.m., what time would I have to leave Targa Train Station?

   _____

8. I am meeting my friend at Tableworth Shopping Center to watch a movie. The movie starts 6:30 p.m. What is the latest time I can leave Targa Train Station and still get there on time?

   _____

9. I am meeting my brother in Novus City for lunch at 1:00 p.m. My closest bus stop is Tidas Road/Gull Street. What is the latest time I could catch the bus there to get to the city on time?

   _____

10. I need to get to Creekville Shopping Center for a performance that begins at 11:00 a.m. What is the latest time I could leave Targa Train Station to get there in time?

   _____

Identifying the Main Idea

Name _____

If you know the main idea of a text, you will have a much better chance of understanding what the content is about.

Activity: Read the passage below and complete pages 26–28.

Surfing

1. Surfing is believed to have been born in Hawaii around CE (AD) 400. It was deeply ingrained in Hawaiian culture, religion, rituals, and beliefs. The first European people to witness surfing were Captain James Cook and his crew in 1788. They documented men surfing on long oval-shaped boards.

2. In 1907, surfing was introduced to California by Henry Huntington. Huntington hired the world's first professional surfer—a Hawaiian native of Irish-Hawaiian descent named George Freeth. Freeth demonstrated surfing in Southern California as part of a promotion for California's Pacific Electric Railway. He earned himself the title of not only California's first surfer, but also the first official lifeguard in the United States.

3. Australians were first introduced to surfing in the summer of 1915, when Hawaiian Olympic medalist by the name of Duke Kahanamoku (also known as "The Duke") visited Freshwater Beach in Sydney. He held a surfing exhibition and demonstrated how to carve a solid surfboard from wood. Isabel Letham was the very first Australian to experience the thrill of surfing when she joined "The Duke" on a tandem surfboard ride.

4. Surfing equipment has developed significantly since the early days of surfing. Boards were originally carved from solid pieces of timber, making them very heavy to carry and not easy to maneuver in the water. They were used until the early 1940s, when they were replaced by hollow plywood surfboards, which were more portable and had increased maneuverability on the wave. Modern surfboards are made from polyurethane foam, wooden stringers to provide strength, fiberglass cloth, and polyester resin. This type of board is stronger and more durable than a hollow plywood board. Surfboard technology is constantly evolving, and a new type of board is starting to hit the market. This board is made of epoxy and is even stronger and lighter and able to be mass-produced. Even more incredible maneuvers will surely be attempted now!

5. Various types of boards are used by surfers:
   - Longboards: around 10 feet in length. They are very stable and make it easy to paddle into and catch waves. However, their size make them difficult and heavy to carry around.
   - Shortboards: just over 6 feet in length. They are also known as "thrusters" and are best suited for experienced surfers. They are very lightweight and easy to maneuver in the waves.
   - Fun boards: around 8 feet in length. They are in between longboards and shortboards and are designed for "fun". Fun boards are quite wide across, making allowances for bigger surfers or those with intermediate skills.
   - A number of niche-type boards are out in the market for experienced surfers that choose to match their skill level, surfing style, and weather conditions.

6. Other equipment used by surfers includes the leash, which basically ties the surfboard to the surfer's leg. This prevents the board from being washed to shore and from hitting other surfers. Surf wax is used for traction and helps to keep the surfer's feet from slipping. Fins, or "skegs," are located on the underside of the surfboard to aid surfing technique. These can either be part of the board or can be attached and changed according to surfing conditions.

7. Surfing is considered by many to be a lifestyle, not a sport, and with millions of people hitting the surf each year, it is a very popular recreational activity for all ages.

Name _____

Follow the steps below to learn how to determine the main idea and why it is imprtant.

- There are often many ideas in a text, but only one idea is the link that joins the other ideas together—this is the main idea.

- Read the text, and then ask yourself, "What is it mainly about?"

- The title is a useful clue to the main idea because a good title often tells the reader what the text is about.

- Always check all possible answers before making a decision.

1. The main idea of *Surfing* is:

    (a) the history of surfing in Australia.

    (b) the different types of surfboards available to modern surfers.

    (c) famous surfers through history.

    (d) the history of surfing and its development over the years.

2. Choose the best answer. Think about each choice carefully.

    (a) One paragraph talks about when surfing was introduced in Australia. However, this is not what the entire text is about. This wouldn't be the best choice.

    (b) Part of the text outlines the development and types of surfboards available to surfers, but this is not the main idea of the entire text. This would not be the best answer.

    (c) The text does mention two famous surfers, but the entire text is not based on this. This would not be the best answer.

    (d) The text does talk about the history of surfing and how it has changed over the years. This is the best answer.

1. The main idea of paragraph 4 is:

    (a) the maneuverability of the surfboard.

    (b) the development of surfboards over time.

    (c) how to make a timber surfboard.

    (d) the use of epoxy when making modern-day surfboards.

2. Choose the best answer. Think about each choice carefully.

    (a) The material from which the surfboard is made affects its maneuverability, but this is not what paragraph 4 is mainly about. This isn't the best answer.

    (b) Paragraph 4 talks about how surfboards have changed and improved over time. This would be a very good answer, but remember to check all answers before choosing one.

    (c) The paragraph doesn't really go into the details of how to make a surfboard from timber. This answer would not be the best choice.

    (d) Yes, epoxy is used when making modern-day surfboards, but this is not the main idea linking all the ideas together in paragraph 4. This would not be the best answer.

Identifying the Main Idea

Name _____

Use the strategies you learned to practice finding the main idea. Use the clues in the "Think!" boxes to help you.

1. What is the main idea of paragraph 1?
   (a) the journey of Captain James Cook
   (b) Hawaiian culture, rituals, beliefs, and religion
   (c) where and when surfing first began, and when it was first witnessed by Europeans
   (d) men surfing on long oval-shaped boards

   > **Think!**
   > What is the single idea that links each sentence together?

2. Which of the following topics would best fit with the main idea of this passage?
   (a) a paragraph about how much surfing lessons cost
   (b) a paragraph about dangerous surfing spots
   (c) a paragraph about other sports similar to surfing
   (d) a paragraph about famous surfers and which types of boards they use

   > **Think!**
   > Read the topics, and ask yourself which one will not change the direction the whole passage is going.

3. The fifth paragraph is mainly about ...

   _____
   _____
   _____

   > **Think!**
   > Look at the lead sentence and the final sentence of the paragraph to help you.

4. State the main idea of paragraph 6.

   _____
   _____
   _____

   > **Think!**
   > Read the paragraph and ask yourself what it is mainly about.

5. Mark an **X** in the box next to the paragraph in which the main idea is contained in the first sentence.

   Paragraph 1 ☐   Paragraph 4 ☐

   Paragraph 2 ☐   Paragraph 5 ☐

   Paragraph 3 ☐   Paragraph 6 ☐

   > **Think!**
   > Read each paragraph and decide what each is mainly about. Then read the first sentence. Does it contain the main idea?

Name _____

Use the strategies you have been practicing to help you identify the main idea.

1. Paragraph 3 is mainly about:

   (a) how and when Australians were first introduced to surfing.

   (b) Duke Kahanamoku, "The Duke," who was a Hawaiian Olympic medalist.

   (c) Miss Isabel Letham, who was the very first Australian to experience the thrill of surfing.

   (d) the great surfing conditions at Freshwater Beach in Sydney.

2. Use the text and your ideas to answer these.

   (a) What is the title of the text?

   _____

   (b) A good title often tells the main idea.

   Do you think this is a good title? ☐ Yes ☐ No

   (c) Explain why you think this.

   _____

   _____

   _____

   _____

   (d) Suggest another title that would be suitable.

   _____

3. Think about the main idea of each paragraph. Write the number of the paragraph where you think each of these statements would best fit.

   (a) "I'm thinking of buying one of the latest epoxy boards to replace my polyurethane foam board." Paragraph ☐

   (b) "Did you know that surfing has been around for more than 1,500 years?" Paragraph ☐

   (c) "My grandfather remembers watching a demonstration on how to carve a solid surfboard from wood." Paragraph ☐

   (d) "What is the purpose of a surfer wearing a leash?" Paragraph ☐

   (e) "My surfing has improved so much that I'm going to try a fun board." Paragraph ☐

Identifying the Main Idea

Name _____

Activity: Read the passage below and complete page 30.

A True Performer

1. Avril Lavigne burst onto the music scene in 2002 at the age of 17, with the release of her debut CD *Let Go*. No one really knew much about her, but she came complete with skater-punk attitude, confidence, and a very strong self-belief.

2. Avril, also known as "Avie" by those close to her, was born in Belleville, Canada on September 27, 1984. At the age of 2, her mother noted that she displayed a talent for singing and performing. She began singing along to songs in church and taught herself how to play the guitar. By the time Avril was in her early teens, she was writing her own songs, playing guitar, and spending as much time as possible singing in front of an audience. When Avril was 13, she won a radio competition to travel to Ottawa and perform a duet with country music star Shania Twain. Over the next few years, Avril experienced a great deal of rejection. She spent a significant amount of time and effort sending videotapes of stage performances to record labels and management companies throughout North America to no avail. But Avril did not give up. Finally, at the age of 16, she caught the eye of a record producer who could see her talent and signed her to a record deal. Her dream was about to become a reality!

3. Avril moved to New York with her older brother as a chaperone to work on her first album at Arista Records. Things weren't working out for Avril in New York, so she moved to Los Angeles and began working with Cliff Magness. Cliff knew how to work with Avril's unique style, and together they completed one of the most successful debut albums of all time. *Let Go* was released on June 4, 2002 and went to number one in Australia, Canada, and the United Kingdom (making her the youngest female soloist to have a number one album in the United Kingdom at that time). The album also went four times platinum, selling 13,197,000 copies worldwide. "Complicated," the debut single, held the number one position for 11 weeks on the Contemporary Hit Radio Chart (used to track the amount of airplay any song receives around the world). Avril was nominated for five Grammy awards, named the best new artist at the MTV Video Music Awards, and received several other awards.

4. After touring and playing to large crowds for two years, Avril settled in Florida and began writing her second album with close friend Chantal Kreviazuk. She had learned a lot over the past two years and had also grown up. Her second album, *Under My Skin*, was released on May 25, 2004 and debuted at number one in the United States, United Kingdom, Germany, Japan, Australia, Canada, Spain, Ireland, Thailand, Korea, and Hong Kong. Her music reached out to a wider audience and her album sold 380,000 copies in the United States in the first week alone. Avril's success is attributed to her determination to stay true to herself—she writes all of her songs based on her own personal experiences. Her talent for singing and songwriting is matched by her musical ability to play guitar, piano, and drums.

5. Avril continued to make successful music albums and even branched out into modeling and acting. She played the voice of Heather the opossum in the animated film *Over the Hedge* and has had several small parts in movies. Avril spends a great deal of her time helping out various charities to support human and health rights issues and helping children who are seriously ill or disadvantaged by war. She is a true example of what pure determination and self-belief can achieve.

Name _____

Use the strategies you learned and practiced in *Surfing* to help you find the main idea.

> **Remember:**
> - The main idea links all the other ideas together and tells what the text is about.
> - Read the text, and then ask yourself, "What is the text mainly about?"
> - Look at the title, too.
> - Read all possible answers carefully before making a decision.

1. What is the main idea of paragraph 2?

   (a) The significance of winning a radio competition.

   (b) The discovery and development of Avril's singing talent.

   (c) Avril's early life and growing up.

   (d) Where Avril Lavigne was born.

> **Think!**
> Read the paragraph, and then consider each possible answer carefully before making a decision.

2. What is the main idea of the last paragraph?

   (a) Avril's current projects and how she works to help the community

   (b) Avril is now becoming an actor and leaving music behind.

   (c) Avril's music career is such a success because of her determination and self-belief.

   (d) Avril works hard doing charity work for the less privileged.

3. Paragraph 3 is mainly about:

   (a) Avril's success working with Cliff Magness.

   (b) The awards Avril received after her debut album.

   (c) Avril's phenomenal success with her debut single and album.

   (d) Avril being named best new artist at the MTV Video Music Awards.

4. State the main idea for these paragraphs.

   (a) Paragraph 1: _____

   _____

   (b) Paragraph 4: _____

   _____

Name _____

Activity: Read the passage below, and use pages 32–34 to show how well you can understand words, find information, and identify main ideas.

Mount Tambora

---

1. Mount Tambora can be found on Sumbawa Island in Indonesia. It is most famous for the site of the most powerful volcanic eruption in recorded history. The VEI is a scale used to measure the intensity of a volcano, determined by the volume of ash erupted from the explosion. The rating begins at zero (non-explosive) all the way to eight (considered to be mega-colossal). The explosion of Mount Tambora was rated 7 on the VEI—four times more powerful than the explosion that destroyed Krakatoa (VEI = 6) in 1883.

2. The word *volcano* originates from the island of Vulcano in the Mediterranean Sea. Long ago, the people in this area thought that Vulcano was the chimney of the forge of Vulcan (the blacksmith of the Roman gods). They believed that the hot lava fragments and clouds of dust erupting from Vulcano came from the forge as Vulcan created thunderbolts for Jupiter (king of the gods) and weapons for Mars (the god of war).

3. A volcano is a vent in the surface of Earth. Magma, gas, and ash erupt through these vents to cause explosions. Six different types of volcanoes exist: shield volcanoes, strato volcanoes, rhyolite caldera complexes, monogenetic fields, flood basalts, and mid-ocean ridges. Mount Tambora is a strato volcano—one of the most common types of volcanoes, and one that is capable of causing the greatest number of casualties and destruction. It is dangerous because the magma builds up inside and causes bulges in the mountain that are then responsible for landslides, avalanches, and lahars (very hot, fast moving lava flows). More often than not, the side of the mountain (flank) will also break away from the pressure that has built up inside.

4. In 1812, Mount Tambora awoke after a long slumber. For three years, locals experienced small eruptions—steam and gas explosions. The first major eruption came on April 5, 1815. A column of gas, ash, and rock rose 15 miles into the sky, but worse was still to come. The main explosion began on April 10, 1815 and continued for five days. Three distinct columns of pyroclastic flow reached 25 miles into the sky. Pyroclastic flows are earth-hugging clouds of hot ash, rocks, and pumice that can kill in minutes. The explosions were heard over 1,600 miles away, and 36 cubic miles of ash erupted and fell as far as 800 miles from Mount Tambora. Roofs of houses 40 miles away collapsed from the weight of the ash, and all vegetation on nearby islands was eradicated. The immense heat caused a huge whirlwind that blew down almost every house in the village. Trees were torn up by their roots and hurled around like toy cars. The eruption also caused a tsunami that recorded a wave height of over 30 feet, which in turn destroyed a number of islands close by. It is estimated that around 10,000 people died immediately as a direct result of the eruption, while another 82,000 people died as a result of starvation and disease caused by the effects of the explosion.

5. The enormous volcanic cloud was responsible for lowering global temperatures by about 5°F. This change in temperature caused farmers to lose crops, which in turn created widespread famine and starvation. The summer of 1816 was called "the year without summer" as parts of Europe and North America were denied their regular summer temperatures. These cooler temperatures were said to be caused by over 200 million tons of sulfur dioxide in the atmosphere, preventing the rays of the sun from reaching Earth's surface. Spectacular sunsets with vivid streaks of green caused by lingering ash in the stratosphere were observed for many years afterwards.

6. On February 28, 2006, scientists found what they believe to be traces of the lost Indonesian civilization of Tambora, which had been completely devastated by the eruption. Researchers from the University of North Carolina, together with the Indonesian Directorate of Volcanology, used ground-penetrating radar to help locate and dig a trench where locals had found ceramics and bones. The researchers managed to unearth what was left of a thatched house, pottery, bronze, and the carbonized bones of two people.

Assessment

Name _____

Remember:
- Find and underline the word or phrase in the text.
- Read that sentence and some of the ones around it to help you to determine the meaning.
- Substitute each answer choice in the sentence to see which one sounds correct.
- Always check all possible answers before making a decision.

---

1. What does the word **intensity** mean? (paragraph 1)

(a) the amount of noise made

(b) the measure of strength or greatness

(c) to experience strong feelings and emotions

(d) being crowded together

2. Explain the meaning of the phrase **researchers managed to unearth**. (paragraph 6)

_____

_____

3. What does the word **casualties** in paragraph 3 mean?

(a) people who are accidentally killed or injured

(b) to be careless

(c) to be informal

(d) something happening by chance

4. Choose the best meaning for the word **eradicated** in paragraph 4.

(a) made even

(b) heated

(c) became radioactive

(d) destroyed

5. What word could best replace **distinct** in paragraph 4?

(a) similar

(b) plain

(c) separate

(d) display

6. Write another word or words that could be used instead of each of these. Paragraph numbers are given to help you locate the words.

(a) **mega-colossal** (1)

_____

(b) **hurled** (4)

_____

(c) **lingering** (5)

_____

(d) **were denied** (5)

_____

Name _____

> **Remember:**
> - Underline keywords in the question to make sure that you know what information you need.
> - Find the keywords in the text, and read the information around them carefully.
> - Always check all possible answers before making a decision.

1. What impact did the volcanic cloud have on the summer of 1816?

   (a) It reduced global temperatures, which caused crops to fail and created widespread famine.

   (b) The United States and Australia missed out on their summer temperatures.

   (c) Farmers took a vacation, which caused widespread famine.

   (d) Numerous animal species became extinct.

2. Explain the VEI scale and its rating system.

   _____

   _____

   _____

3. Which type of volcano is capable of causing the most casualties?

   (a) shield

   (b) monogenetic field

   (c) mid-ocean ridge

   (d) strato

4. Mount Tambora is famous for:

   (a) being an island in Indonesia.

   (b) being a strato volcano.

   (c) causing a tsunami.

   (d) being the most powerful volcanic eruption in recorded history.

5. Explain the importance of the find that occurred on February 28, 2006.

   _____

   _____

   _____

   _____

Name _____

Remember:
- The main idea links all the other ideas together and tells what the text is mainly about.
- The title is an excellent clue to the main idea of the text.
- Always check all possible answers before making a decision.

---

1. What is the main idea of the third paragraph?

   (a) outlining the different types of volcanoes

   (b) explaining what happens during a volcanic eruption

   (c) explaining where the name *volcano* originated

   (d) explaining what a volcano is and the different types of volcanoes

2. What is the main idea of the fourth paragraph?

   (a) outlining the events of the Mount Tambora explosion and the devastating impact

   (b) to explain what pyroclastic flows are

   (c) to discuss the impact of a large volcano on the surrounding areas

   (d) to show how destructive volcanoes can be

3. Explain the main idea of paragraph 1.

   _____

   _____

4. Use the text and your ideas to answer these.

   (a) What is the title of the text? _____

   (b) A good title often tells the main idea.

   Is this a good title? ☐ Yes   ☐ No

   (c) Explain why you think this. _____

   _____

   (d) Suggest another title that would be suitable. _____

   _____

5. State the main idea of paragraph 6.

   _____

   _____

Lesson Objective

- Students will sequence events.

Background Information

This section demonstrates how to determine the order in which events occur, sometimes using time markers and other strategies to identify the relationship between events.

Knowing the sequence of events is an important and often critical factor in a reader's understanding of a text.

First, students need to determine from the question which events they are required to sequence. Then, they should locate them in the text and look for any time-marker words that could be helpful. Examples could include: *before, then, when, while, after, finally, at last,* or *following.*

Students may also find creating timelines of sections of the text or specific events a useful strategy.

Activity Answers

Fun with the Dunns .... **Pages 39–42**

- Practice Page: Page 41
    1. (c)
    2. (d)
    3. 4, 3, 2, 5, 1
    4. Eleanor began to cry on cue and then smiled at Jake who clenched his fists, got up, and headed for the back door.
- On Your Own: Page 42
    1. (b)
    2. He glared at Imogen and Eleanor, he raised his eyebrows, he slumped into the chair, and he wrinkled his brow.
    3. (a)
    4. Answers will vary.
    5. First: "No, I have to practice my violin."
       Last: "Where are you going?"

Writing a Spy Novel.. **Pages 43–44**

- Try It Out: Page 44
    1. (c)
    2. She reads the manuscript through, jotting notes on a separate sheet of paper. Then, she takes several months to edit the manuscript and finally sends it to her publisher.
    3. (d)
    4. 3, 2, 5, 1, 4

Assessment Answers

Sequencing..**Page 58**

    1. (c)
    2. The paintings were sold for millions of dollars; The twins disappeared; The twins' parents received letters from Isabel.
    3. (d)
    4. 4, 2, 3, 1

Lesson Objective

- Students will compare and contrast people, places, and events.

same	different

T–chart

Background Information

The ability to compare and contrast the information provided in a text enhances the reader's understanding of that text and is an important comprehension skill students need to practice.

Students are required to categorize information in order to determine what some people, places, and events have in common or how they differ.

Graphic organizers are very useful tools for identifying similarities and differences, particularly Venn diagrams, T–charts, and compare-and-contrast charts.

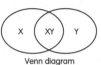

Venn diagram

A	B	A	B
compare		contrast	

Compare-and-Contrast chart

Activity Answers

Leopards and Cheetahs .... **Pages 45–48**

- Practice Page: Page 47

1. (c)

	Cheetah	Leopard
Hunt at night		✗
Fastest land animal	✗	
Tear stain	✗	
Store kill in trees		✗
Eat meat	✗	✗

2. (a)

Leopards / **Cheetahs**
hunt at night, store kill in trees / eat meat / fastest land animal, tear stain

(b) eat meat

3. They both stalk their prey to get as close as possible so they don't have to run for long.

4. Answers should include three of the following: leopards are larger, have shorter legs, have rosettes instead of spots, don't have a "tear stain" mark, have a larger head, and can retract their claws.

- On Your Own: Page 48

1. (c)   2. (b)

3. Cheetahs and leopards both climb trees to keep watch for prey. Leopards also climb trees to rest or to store their prey.

4. "tear stain" mark—to reduce glare; non-retractable claws—help them grip the ground when they are running; a lean body—to increase their speed; large nasal passages—helps them take in more air when recovering after a kill

5. cheetah; quickly; large cats, hyenas, or other scavengers might drive them away; leopard; it is strong enough to drag its prey into a tree to store it for later consumption.

Bigfoot? .... **Pages 49–50**

- Try It Out: Page 50

1. (d)   2. (c)

3. They were both collecting sticks, stood/walked on two legs, and shrieked and ran when frightened.

4. The writer of Account 1 stood frozen to the spot at first then tried to get his camera. He called out to the creature and chased after it, and then finally took some photographs of its footprints. The writer of Account 2 also felt frozen after leaping to his feet and called out to the creature but didn't take any photographs or chase the creature.

5. The creature from Account 1 had long, shaggy fur, a short neck, facial features like a gorilla and smelled like a pungent curry, whereas the creature from Account 2 had short, fuzzy fur, a long neck, facial features like an orangutan, and smelled like strong perfume.

Assessment Answers

Finding Similarities and Differences .... **Page 59**

1. (c)   2. (c)

3. The first art expert had been offered money by the twins to be part of their hoax, so he declared the paintings to be genuine. The second art expert correctly declared the paintings to be fakes.

4. (a) Belinda   (b) Isabel   (c) Belinda and Isabel   (d) Belinda

Lesson Objective

- Students will use information from a text to predict outcomes not explicitly stated in the text.

Background Information

To be able to predict outcomes, often in terms of the probable actions or reactions of specific characters, students need to focus on content and understand what they read. They need to monitor their understanding as they read, constantly confirming, rejecting, or adjusting their predictions.

The focus of this section is on teaching students how to locate and use the information provided in the text to determine probable outcomes and then to evaluate their predictions.

Students need to be able to locate specific information related to an issue and/or characters, using keywords and concepts. Their predictions should not be wild guesses, but well-thought-out, relevant ideas based on the information provided and some prior knowledge.

If students' answers differ, it is suggested that they check again to see why their answer varies from the one given. If they can justify their answer, teachers may decide to accept it.

Activity Answers

Lost! ....Pages 51–54

- Practice Page: Page 53
    1. (c)
    2. (b)
    3. Answers should indicate that Flynn would not be pleased about it.
    4. Answers could indicate that Megan would probably try to get to the horse again.
- On Your Own: Page 54
    1. (d)
    2. Answers should indicate that Flynn would not be happy about it, but Aaron would like to go.
    3. (a)
    4. Answers will vary.

Moonlight Forest ....Pages 55–56

- Try It Out: Page 56
    1. (b)
    2. (c)
    3. Answers will vary. Answers could indicate that Mr. Johns seems to be a joker, so Ella's costume will probably end up being close to what she wants.
    4. (b)
    5. Answers will vary.

Assessment Answers

Predicting ....Page 60

1. (a)
2. Answers will vary.
3. Answers will vary.
4. (b)

Helpful Hints

SEQUENCING

- Make sure you know which events you need to sequence. Then find those events in the text.

- Pay attention to how they are related. Making a mental picture of what is happening in the text sometimes helps you imagine the sequence.

- Always check all possible answers before deciding on your answer.

FINDING SIMILARITIES AND DIFFERENCES

- Make sure you understand the question before you begin. Then find the keywords.

- Use a chart, table, Venn diagram, or other type of organizer, if you need to. This will help you find similarities and differences.

- Always check all possible answers before deciding on your answer.

PREDICTING

- You need to find the information that connects to the question.

- The answer will not be found in the text, but there is information you can use and think about as you read. The writer will suggest, rather than tell, what is likely to happen. You must use the details in the text to help you predict.

- Always check all possible answers before deciding on your answer.

Sequencing

Name _____

To fully understand what you read, you must be able to determine the order in which events happen. This is called *sequencing*.

Activity: Read the story below and complete pages 40–42.

Fun with the Dunns

1. "But I don't want to go!" I said. "Please, Mom, don't make me. Please?"

2. "You have to go," said Mom, putting down her lipstick. "I certainly can't let you stay here on your own. You know what happened last time your father and I went out—and that was just for half an hour."

3. "They were accidents!" I said. "Letting the bath overflow and blowing up the microwave could have happened to anyone."

4. "Anyone named Jake, that is." Mom pursed her lips. "No, sorry, Jake. Your father and I are going out to have a nice lunch with Mr. and Mrs. Dunn, and you can stay with Imogen and Eleanor. It will only be for a few hours."

5. And that's why, a short time later, I was standing in the Dunns' family room with their horrible daughters. Imogen was 16 and was only interested in talking about boys on the phone to her friends. Eleanor was my age, and she hardly talked at all except to boss people around. I glared at both of them.

6. "I'll be on the phone in my room if either of you need me," said Imogen. She flounced out. Hopefully that would be the last I'd see of her for the day. That just left Eleanor. She was looking me up and down.

7. "Is it okay if I watch TV?" I asked hopefully.

8. "No," she said. "I have to practice my violin."

9. I raised my eyebrows. "Do you have to do it in here?" I said.

10. "Whose house is this?" she asked. "I'll practice wherever I like." She turned her back to me and picked up her violin case off the floor.

11. "Fine," I said. "I'll read a book."

12. "I hope you brought your own," said Eleanor, plucking the violin strings. "Because I'm not lending you any of mine."

13. I really couldn't stand her. I slumped onto the lounge chair.

14. "Don't sit there," she said. "That's Dad's favorite chair."

15. "Don't be ridiculous!" I said.

16. "Okay," she said. "Sit there and then when your mom and dad come back, I'll start crying and say that you were mean to me."

17. I wrinkled my brow. Surely nobody could cry on cue? Just as I thought this, her lip trembled and a tear started rolling down her cheek. She smiled. "It's a little talent of mine."

18. That did it. I couldn't stand to be in the room with this girl anymore. I clenched my fists, got up, and headed for the back door.

19. "Where are you going?" Eleanor called.

20. "None of your business," I snarled. "Just leave me alone."

Name _____

Follow the steps below to learn how to determine the sequence of events.

- The order in which things happen is very important.
- Make sure you understand which events you need to sequence.
- Look in the text to find the events listed as possible answers and underline them.
- You will need to determine how these events are related. There may be some time-marker words, such as *then*, *before*, or *next*, in the text to help you.
- Always check all possible answers before making a decision.

1. Which event happened *after* Eleanor smiled?

   (a) Eleanor's lip trembled.

   (b) Jake spoke for the first time.

   (c) Imogen spoke.

   (d) Jake headed for the back door.

2. Choose the best answer. Think about each choice carefully.

   (a) Eleanor's lip trembled just before she smiled (paragraph 17). This is not a good answer.

   (b) Jake spoke for the first time right at the beginning of the text. This is not the best answer.

   (c) Imogen only spoke once in paragraph 6, about halfway through the text. This cannot be a good answer.

   (d) Jake did head for the back door after Eleanor smiled. This must be the best answer.

1. What happened just *before* Eleanor plucked the violin strings?

   (a) Imogen flounced out of the room.

   (b) Eleanor picked up her violin case.

   (c) Jake said that he would read a book.

   (d) Jake wrinkled his brow.

2. Choose the best answer. Think about each choice carefully.

   (a) Many events take place between Imogen flouncing out of the room and Eleanor plucking the violin strings. This is unlikely to be a good answer.

   (b) Eleanor did pick up her violin case not long before she plucked the strings. This could be the answer.

   (c) Jake said that he would read a book just before Eleanor plucked the violin strings. This is the best answer.

   (d) Jake wrinkled his brow (paragraph 17) after Eleanor plucked the violin strings. This could not be the best answer.

Sequencing

Name _____

Use the strategies you learned to practice sequencing. Use the clues in the "Think!" boxes to help you.

1. Which event took place *first*?

    (a) Jake told Eleanor not to be ridiculous.

    (b) Eleanor looked Jake up and down.

    (c) Jake glared at Eleanor and Imogen.

    (d) Jake slumped onto the lounge chair.

> **Think!**
> You may need to scan the text and underline each event to find out which one took place *first*.

2. Which of these events happened *between* Jake's mom pursing her lips and Jake asking if he could watch TV?

    (a) Jake said, "Do you have to do it in here?"

    (b) Jake felt he couldn't stand to be in the room with Eleanor anymore.

    (c) Jake said, "But I don't want to go!"

    (d) Jake's mom mentioned lunch with Mr. and Mrs. Dunn.

> **Think!**
> Find the part of the text that describes Jake's mom and the part that describes Jake asking if he could watch TV, and then read what happened in between to determine the answer.

3. Put these events in order by using the numbers 1 to 5.

    [ ] Eleanor turned her back to Jake.

    [ ] Imogen left the room.

    [ ] Jake admitted he had blown up the microwave.

    [ ] Jake clenched his fists.

    [ ] Jake's mom told him he couldn't stay in their house on his own.

> **Think!**
> You will need to find all of these events in the text to determine the order in which they happened.

4. Explain the events that took place after Jake wrinkled his brow.

_____

_____

_____

_____

> **Think!**
> Find this event in the text and read the sentences after it.

Name _____

Use the strategies you have been practicing to help you determine the sequence of events.

1. What happened last?

   (a) Jake thought that nobody could cry on cue.

   (b) Jake snarled at Eleanor.

   (c) Jake's mom told him that she and his father were going out to lunch.

   (d) Eleanor threatened to tell Jake's mom and dad that he had been mean to her if he didn't get off the chair.

2. Apart from speaking, list four things that Jake did at the Dunns' house before the tear rolled down Eleanor's cheek.

   • _____

   • _____

   • _____

   • _____

3. What was Eleanor's first response to Jake asking if she had to practice her violin in the family room?

   (a) "Whose house is this?"

   (b) She showed him how she could pretend to cry.

   (c) "I hope you brought your own."

   (d) "I'll practice wherever I like."

4. Describe two events, in order, that took place between the two listed below.

   • Jake said he didn't want to go to the Dunns' house.

   • _____

   _____

   • _____

   _____

   • Jake stood in the Dunns' family room.

5. Write the first and last statements Eleanor said.

   First: _____

   Last: _____

42

Sequencing

Name _____

Activity: Read the story below and complete page 44.

Writing a Spy Novel

1. As a well-known author, many people have asked me about the process I use to write one of my spy novels. Here is an example of my usual routine.

2. Once I have a basic story idea in my head, I literally go in search of the main characters. I visit public places where I find lots of people—train stations, shopping centers, and parks. I then watch for people who may fit my story idea. I take note of how they walk, how they speak, and what they are wearing. After a few hours, I come home with plenty of ideas. I give the characters names, think up backgrounds and family details for them, and write their details into a notebook. Often, I will mix up the characteristics of the people I observed and merge them into one character.

3. Next, I expand on my plot by drawing a cluster diagram. Some people may know this as a "mind map." In the middle of a large sheet of paper, I write the working title of my novel in a circle. Then, I draw lines out from the title and in more circles, I write the names of the locations and main events that I want to create in the novel. Then, I pin the sheet of paper to a corkboard above my desk so I can see it easily as I write. Around it, I pin the character notes I wrote earlier.

4. Now you might think I would actually start writing—but I don't! At this stage, I always go for a long walk. I take a voice recorder with me. As I walk, I visualize the events of my novel as if it were a movie and talk into the recorder to help record the most vivid images. Sometimes, I even suggest which famous actors I would choose to play each of the main characters if my spy novel were to be made into a movie.

5. Once I return from my walk, I sketch some of the important scenes I visualized. I am very lucky that I can draw as well as write—I would be quite lost if I couldn't! Once all of this is in place, I then try to forget about my plans for the novel for about a week. Then, when I get back to my desk, I can consider everything I have written or drawn with a fresh eye. Sometimes, I am horrified by some of my weak ideas, or I spot a huge hole in the plot. I always feel that this week off is worth it.

6. Now I begin writing! I work on a computer with a large screen, so I can see two pages at a time. I don't write my novels in order because I find that idea quite daunting. Instead, I write the most exciting scenes first; the ones I can visualize most clearly. This helps to keep me interested. I only have one rule—I always write the ending last. This is because I almost always change my original ending while I am writing.

7. Once I have written all the scenes, I then put them in order. This is a long and tedious task. I really don't enjoy this aspect of creating a novel, but it is the price I pay for writing out of order! Once it is together, I read it through. I don't allow myself to make any changes on this first reading, but I do jot notes on a separate sheet of paper as ideas occur to me.

8. After this stage, it is time for editing. This takes me several months. Then finally, the manuscript is sent to my publisher. I keep my fingers crossed that they—and my loyal readers—will like it!

Name _____

Use the strategies you learned and practiced in *Fun with the Dunns* to help you determine the sequence of events.

> **Remember:**
> • Make sure you know which events you need to sequence.
> • Find and underline them in the text.
> • Determine how they are related. Look for time-marker words.
> • Check all possible answers before making a decision.

1. Which of these things does the author do before she draws a cluster diagram?

(a) She goes for a walk.

(b) She makes a mind map.

(c) She watches people.

(d) She starts writing the novel.

> **Think!**
> Find the part of the text that describes the author drawing a cluster diagram to find out what happens before.

2. Explain what the author does after putting her scenes in order.

_____

_____

_____

_____

3. Which of these things occurs between the author returning from her walk and beginning to write?

(a) She pins up her character notes on a corkboard.

(b) She talks into a voice recorder.

(c) She writes the most exciting scene.

(d) She draws some of the scenes she visualized.

4. Use the numbers 1 to 5 to show the order in which these events happen in the text.

☐ The author takes a week off.

☐ The author pins the cluster diagram to a corkboard.

☐ The author edits the manuscript.

☐ The author writes character details in a notebook.

☐ The author writes the ending of the novel.

Finding Similarities and Differences

Name _____

To help you understand what you read in a text, you sometimes need to think about how things are alike or how they are different and make comparisons.

Activity: Read the passage below and complete pages 46–48.

Leopards and Cheetahs

1. Leopards and cheetahs are members of the cat family. Because they both have spotted coats, many people confuse them.

2. Leopards live in Africa and some parts of Asia. The adults are solitary animals. They are found in rainforests, mountains, grasslands, and even deserts. Leopards prefer to live in shaded areas with some cover, such as rocks or dense foliage, to hide in or behind. Most leopards are a tan color with flower-shaped spots called *rosettes*. Like lions, tigers, and jaguars, leopards can roar. They also purr when they are content.

3. Like all cats, leopards are meat-eaters. They hunt at night for their prey, which may include baboons, large birds, antelope, and even porcupines. They may also hunt for fish, because unlike other cats, they are strong swimmers. Leopards can run quickly (reaching 36 miles per hour in short bursts), but they don't chase their prey over long distances, preferring instead to stalk and then pounce, grabbing it with their retractable claws. Leopards are incredibly strong. They can drag the large animals they have hunted up trees to eat or store for later consumption. Leopards will often climb trees to rest or keep watch for prey.

4. Unfortunately, leopards are endangered largely due to humans hunting them for their fur. In some areas, farmers think of leopards as pests.

5. Cheetahs are smaller and lighter than leopards. Their legs are also longer in proportion to their bodies. They are a tan color, with a pattern of black solid spots on their coats. Their heads are smaller in proportion to their bodies in comparison to a leopard's, and they have a characteristic black "tear stain" on their faces, running from the corner of the eye to the mouth. This is thought to be an adaptation that helps deflect the sun's glare from their eyes. Unlike other cats, cheetahs cannot retract their claws fully, using them for grip while running. Cheetahs can make a variety of sounds, including purring and a unique bird-like "chirp." However, unlike other big cats, they cannot roar.

6. Cheetahs live in Africa. They are endangered, largely due to habitat loss and because humans hunt them for their fur. Cheetahs are generally solitary animals but are sometimes found living in small groups. They live in grasslands and open plains where prey is abundant. They will sometimes climb trees to keep watch for prey.

7. Cheetahs are the fastest land animal on Earth and are truly built for speed, having very little fat on their bodies compared to that of a leopard. Cheetahs can reach speeds of about 70 miles per hour—but only in short bursts. This means they must stalk their prey, aiming to get as close as possible before having to sprint. Cheetahs hunt during the day, mainly preying on young or small antelope. They are the only cat that can turn in mid-air while running. Cheetahs have larger nasal passages than other cats—an adaptation that helps them to take in more air while they are recovering after catching their prey. They are not strong enough to hide or guard their catch, so they eat the meat quickly before a larger cat, hyena, or other scavenger drives them away from their meal. Because of this, cheetahs hunt much more often than leopards, who often store their prey.

8. So based on the descriptions of leopards and cheetahs that you read, which animal do you think is pictured above?

Name _____

Follow the steps below to learn how to organize information to make it easier to answer questions about similarities and differences.

- Make sure you understand the question and underline the keywords.
- Sometimes, it is easy to see how things are different or the same if you are comparing two things. However, if there are three or more things to compare, it can be helpful to organize the information in a chart. Two examples are shown below.
- Always check all possible answers before making a decision.

1. Which two things do cheetahs and leopards have in common?

   (a) They are meat-eaters, and they hunt during the day.

   (b) They can purr, and they have retractable claws.

   (c) They have retractable claws, and they hunt during the day.

   (d) They are meat-eaters, and they can purr.

	Leopard	Cheetah
Meat-eater		
Purrs		
Retractable claws		
Hunts during the day		

2. Choose the best answer. Think about each choice carefully. You will find it useful to complete the chart above first and use it to find the best answer.

   (a) Both cats are meat-eaters, but only cheetahs hunt during the day. This is not a good answer.

   (b) Both cats can purr, but only the leopard has retractable claws. This cannot be the best answer.

   (c) Only the leopard has retractable claws, and only the cheetah hunts during the day. This is not a good answer.

   (d) Both cats are meat-eaters and can purr. This is the best answer.

---

1. Use the information in the Venn diagram to help you find the answer.

   The leopard and the cheetah both:

   (a) are night hunters and purr.

   (b) are endangered and have solid black spots.

   (c) are tan and can climb trees.

   (d) are day hunters and eat meat.

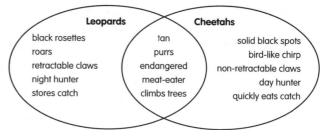

2. Choose the best answer. Think about each choice carefully.

   (a) The leopard is a night hunter, but not the cheetah. This is not a good answer.

   (b) Both animals are endangered, but only the cheetah has solid black spots. This is not a good answer.

   (c) Both animals are tan and can climb trees. This is a very good answer, but check all answers.

   (d) Only the cheetah is a day hunter, so this is not a good answer.

Finding Similarities and Differences

Name _____

Use the strategies you learned to practice finding similarities and differences. Use the clues in the "Think!" boxes to help you.

1. Refer to the text to complete the chart, which in turn will help you to answer this question.

Which two things are only true of leopards?

(a) They hunt at night, and they are the fastest land animal on Earth.

(b) They are the fastest land animal on Earth, and they have a "tear stained" face.

(c) They store their kill high in a tree, and they hunt at night.

(d) They have a "tear stained" face, and they store their kill high in a tree.

	Cheetah	Leopard
Hunt at night		
Fastest land animal		
Tear stain		
Store kill in trees		
Eat meat		

2. (a) Complete the Venn diagram to show the information in the chart above.

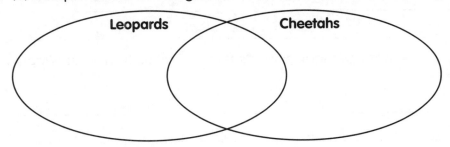

Leopards   Cheetahs

> ## Think!
> You will not need to refer to the text. The information you need should be on the chart you completed above.

(b) What do both animals do? _____

3. What is similar about the way leopards and cheetahs catch their prey?

_____

_____

_____

_____

> ## Think!
> Refer to the text. You may not need to use a chart to help you complete questions 3 and 4.

4. List three ways in which leopards differ in their appearance from cheetahs.

• _____

• _____

• _____

Name _____

Use the strategies you have been practicing to help you identify similarities and differences. You can draw a chart or Venn diagram on a separate sheet of paper if needed.

1. What is one difference between leopards and cheetahs?

   (a) Cheetahs are always solitary animals.

   (b) Leopards are not solitary animals.

   (c) Cheetahs sometimes live in small groups.

   (d) Leopards sometimes live in small groups.

2. Which two things do leopards and cheetahs have in common?

   (a) They are considered pests, and they eat antelope.

   (b) They eat antelope, and they are endangered.

   (c) They are endangered, and they are strong swimmers.

   (d) They are strong swimmers, and they are killed as pests.

3. Explain the different reasons why cheetahs and leopards climb trees.

   _____

   _____

   _____

4. List four special adaptations cheetahs have that leopards do not. Explain how each adaptation helps the cheetah.

   • _____

   _____

   • _____

   _____

   • _____

   _____

   • _____

   _____

5. Complete the sentence to show one difference in the way leopards and cheetahs handle their prey.

   A _____ must eat its prey _____ because _____

   _____

   _____ ,

   whereas a _____ doesn't have to because _____

   _____

   _____ .

Finding Similarities and Differences

Name _____

Actvity: Read the journal entries below and complete page 50.

Bigfoot?

Account 1—July 11, 2003

1.   I was on a camping vacation in the forest, when I saw the creature called "Bigfoot." It was early morning, about 6 a.m., and the sun was just rising. I had bent down to light a campfire to boil some water for a cup of tea, when I heard some rustling in the bushes behind me. I stood up and whirled around, afraid it might be a bear. But instead, I was awestruck to see a giant ape-like creature. It stood on two legs and was much taller than an adult human. I would guess it was about 10 feet tall. It was covered in reddish, long, shaggy fur and had a large head with facial features like those of a gorilla. It had a very short neck. The creature appeared to be collecting sticks that it tucked under its arm as it walked. It moved slowly and steadily on its long, powerful legs.

2.   I must have stood frozen in the spot for about 20 minutes, watching the creature. I was downwind of it, and I smelled a strong odor—similar to a pungent curry. Finally, I thought to get my digital camera. I slid sideways towards my tent, but unfortunately, I stepped on a twig, which cracked loudly. Although the creature was some distance away, it heard my ruckus. It turned its head and looked directly at me with terrified eyes. I called out, trying to reassure it, but it let out an ear-piercing shriek, dropped its sticks, and began to run. I chased after it, but it must have been going at twice my speed, and I soon lost it. I returned to the place where it had dropped the sticks and looked at its footprints. I could fit three of my feet into one of its prints. It also had four toes on each foot. I took some photographs and then packed up camp and headed to the ranger's station to explain what I had seen. However, no one would believe me. Nevertheless, I will never forget what I saw that day.

Account 2—July 15, 2003

3.   I was hiking through the forest when I saw some huge, four-toed footprints. I had just bent down to study them, when I heard a yelping sound. I looked up and found myself face to face with an ape-like creature. Its fur was a reddish color and short and fuzzy. It had facial features like those of an orangutan and a long neck. I leaped to my feet, and the creature did the same. It towered over me, and I am not a short man. It had a ferocious look on its face, and I was sure it wanted to eat me. I wanted to run, but I felt frozen. As I stood there, I could smell a curious odor from the creature. It wasn't unpleasant—it resembled strong perfume.

4.   The creature raised its hand. It was clutching a bundle of sticks, and I yelled in fear. Then, to my surprise, the creature placed its hand on my head and patted it. Its expression had changed to one of curiosity. It regarded me with its head tilted to one side. Then, it backed away slowly, grunted, and strode away on its two long legs. I wanted to call out to it, but I didn't want to frighten it. I suddenly remembered that I had my camera in my pocket, and I dug it out and aimed it at the creature. At that moment, it glanced over its shoulder and saw what I was doing. It shrieked and began to run, still clutching the sticks.

5.   "Wait!" I called, but the creature was disappearing into the trees. I marveled at its speed. I didn't even attempt to chase it.

6.   I wish I had some pictures of that day to prove what I saw. It was unforgettable.

Finding Similarities and Differences

Name _____

Use the strategies you learned and practiced in *Leopards and Cheetahs* to help you recognize similarities and differences. Remember to use charts or Venn diagrams if you need to.

> **Remember:**
> - Make sure you understand the question and underline the keywords.
> - Use a chart or Venn diagram if you need to.
> - Check all possible answers before making a decision.

1. The creatures in the journal entries are the same because:
   (a) they both have long, shaggy hair.
   (b) they both have large eyes.
   (c) they both have long necks.
   (d) they both have four toes on each foot.

> **Think!**
> Try to find each answer in both parts of the text.

2. Which two things do the accounts have in common?
   (a) They take place in the forest, and the writer took photographs.
   (b) The writer took photographs, and the creature patted him on the head.
   (c) They both take place in the forest and occur in 2003.
   (d) They both occur in 2003, and the creature pats the writer on the head.

3. Write three things the creatures did that were similar.

   • _____
   _____

   • _____
   _____

   • _____
   _____

4. Compare the different actions the two writers took when they saw the creatures.

   _____
   _____
   _____
   _____

5. List four differences between the way the creatures looked and smelled.

   • _____

   • _____

   • _____

   • _____

Predicting

Name _____

As we read, it is important to think about what is happening and to predict what we think may happen next.

Activity: Read the story below and complete pages 52–54.

Lost!

1. "Now wait right here and look after Megan. We'll only be a few minutes."

2. Flynn watched his mom and dad disappear into the souvenir shop. He sighed. He was getting really sick of walking around cities on this vacation. Why couldn't they spend an afternoon hanging out at the hotel just watching free inhouse movies? That would be much more fun than looking at boring historical sites and museums. He glanced at his brother, who was happily taking photographs of a fountain. Aaron loved history, just like their parents.

3. Megan was grasping Flynn's hand tightly. "Horsie!" she called out, pointing to a horse and carriage trotting down the street.

4. "Yeah, big deal." Megan was only three, but she was so annoying, always chattering away—often to animals and complete strangers, much to his mom's horror.

5. "Horsie!" Suddenly, Megan wrenched her hand away and took off down the street after the carriage. In an instant, she'd disappeared around the corner.

6. "Megan!" Flynn yelled. He tapped Aaron on the shoulder. "Help me get her!" He took off with Aaron hot on his heels.

7. "Not again," he heard Aaron mutter behind him. Flynn wasn't sure if he was referring to Megan taking off or him neglecting to look after her properly. He didn't have time to think too much as he darted through a group of people and rounded the corner.

8. There was no sign of Megan.

9. "Where is she?" Flynn could feel familiar panic rising. A million plans flashed through his mind. Should they go back and find their parents? Should he and Aaron split up and hunt down different streets? Should they…?

10. "Flynn." Aaron's sensible voice brought him to his senses. "Here's what we'll do. She could only have gone in two directions—either farther along this street or down the alleyway. I'll take the alleyway. I'll meet you back here in five minutes."

11. Flynn nodded. He looked at his watch and then ran off down the street, dodging the crowd. The street came to a dead end after about 100 yards. He turned back. A sick feeling hit him. What if someone had kidnapped her?

12. "Flynn!" He squinted ahead and saw Aaron waving at him. Megan was by his side, grinning.

13. Flynn jogged up to them. He felt sudden anger boil up inside him, and he screamed at her. "Megan! Don't you dare run off like that again!"

14. Her face turned red, and she started to bawl. She clung to Aaron, and he picked her up and cuddled her. He shook his head and rolled his eyes at Flynn and walked past him around the corner back to their parents. They were standing outside the souvenir shop with worried looks on their faces.

15. Flynn just knew he'd be in trouble again.

Learning Page

Name _____

Follow the steps below to learn how to make a prediction about what may happen next.

- The answers are not found in the text, but there is information for you to use and think about.
- You need to find information related to the question. (This could be underlined.)
- Think hard! What is the writer suggesting might happen?
- Always consider all possible answers before making a decision.

1. Which of these things are Flynn's parents most likely to say to him when they first find out that Megan ran away?

(a) "Are you having a good day?"

(b) "Isn't Megan naughty?"

(c) "I'm sure you feel bad about Megan running away."

(d) "Flynn! Why weren't you watching Megan?"

2. Choose the best answer. Think about each choice carefully.

(a) Flynn's parents are unlikely to make such a casual comment after finding out that their daughter had run away. This is not a good answer.

(b) Flynn's parents will probably think that Flynn is at least partly to blame for Megan running away, so they are unlikely to say such a thing.

(c) Flynn's parents will probably want Flynn to explain how Megan got away. They would not likely empathize with how he is feeling. This is not the answer.

(d) Flynn's parents would want an explanation for Megan's disappearance. They are feeling worried, so they will probably speak sharply to Flynn. This is the best answer.

1. Which of these things would Megan most likely do if she saw a dog and its owner?

(a) hide behind her mother

(b) watch the dog

(c) run over and talk to them

(d) scream in terror

2. Choose the best answer. Think about each choice carefully.

(a) The text suggests that Megan is confident for a three-year-old, and she likes animals. This is not a good answer.

(b) Megan obviously likes animals, so she might just watch the dog. However, when she saw the horse, she ran up to it. This is not a likely answer.

(c) When Megan saw the horse, she ran over to it. The text also says that she likes to chatter to animals and people. This is a good answer.

(d) Megan was not frightened to run up to a horse—a much larger animal than a dog. The text also says she likes chattering to animals. This is not a likely answer.

Predicting

Name _____

Use the strategies you learned to help you predict what will happen. Use the clues in the "Think!" boxes to help you.

1. Which of these things is most likely to happen the day after the story finishes?

   (a) The family would do whatever Megan wanted to do.

   (b) The family would spend an afternoon at the hotel watching movies.

   (c) The family would visit a historical site or museum.

   (d) The family would look at horses.

   > **Think!**
   > Consider what most members of the family are enjoying on this vacation.

2. How might Megan behave towards Flynn for the rest of the day?

   (a) She would want him to cuddle with her.

   (b) She would stay away from him.

   (c) She would tease him to get a reaction out of him.

   (d) She would want him to look after her again.

   > **Think!**
   > Read about how Megan reacted when Flynn screamed at her.

3. What would Flynn most likely say and do if his parents were to ask him to look after Megan again?

   _____

   _____

   _____

   _____

   > **Think!**
   > Read about how Flynn reacted to Megan running away.

4. If Megan were to see the horse again, what do you think would happen?

   _____

   _____

   _____

   _____

   _____

   _____

   > **Think!**
   > Consider Megan's personality and what she did the first time she saw the horse.

Name _____

Use the strategies you have been practicing to help you make predictions about what may happen.

1. Most likely, what would have happened if Aaron hadn't been nearby when Megan ran away?

   (a) Megan would have ran back to their parents.

   (b) Flynn would have checked the alleyway.

   (c) Megan would have found Flynn.

   (d) Flynn would have panicked.

2. Explain how you think both Aaron and Flynn would react to their parents suggesting they go on a walking tour of the historical parts of the city that afternoon.

   _____

   _____

   _____

   _____

   _____

3. Which of these things would most likely have happened if the boys hadn't found Megan within five minutes?

   (a) Aaron would have come up with another plan.

   (b) They would have checked the alleyway and the street again.

   (c) Flynn would have told Aaron to go away.

   (d) Megan would have found her way back to the souvenir shop.

4. Explain what you think Aaron will do once the boys reach their parents and what Flynn's reaction might be.

   _____

   _____

   _____

   _____

   _____

   _____

   _____

Name _____

Activity: Read the diary entry below and complete page 56.

Moonlight Forest

Dear Diary,

1. It's almost here! Tomorrow is the opening night of "Moonlight Forest." Even though I have acted in so many of our community theater group's plays before, this is the first time I have had the lead role.

2. I usually feel quite confident about acting, but this time I am really nervous. When I get nervous, my mind tends to go blank. I am so worried that I will forget all of my lines. Mrs. Sinclair, the acting coach, says that is ridiculous. She says that I have only ever forgotten one line at a rehearsal—and that didn't matter because I covered it so well! I suppose she's right—I've taken acting classes for so many years that I can make things up on the spot. But I still worry about it!

3. The other thing I worry about is the costumes. I haven't even tried mine on yet! Mr. Johns, who is in charge of costumes and props, has been sick for the last two days and hasn't been able to get to the theater. My costume is supposed to be a fairy dress. I am hoping for a long, floaty dress in a pale color, but the last time I hinted about that to Mr. Johns, he wrinkled up his nose and said that he had a "much better idea" for my costume. He then talked loudly to the other cast members about how much he liked tutus and bright colors. My stomach dropped to my knees. I hope he was joking.

4. The thing I worry about least is the other actors. Most of them are very experienced, and I know they'll help me out if something goes wrong on stage. Mr. Johns, who apart from doing props and costumes, is also playing a goblin. He sometimes makes up lines as he goes along as a joke, but I overheard Mrs. Sinclair warning him not to do that this time. The only person I worry about in the cast is Jeremy. He's six years old, and he's playing an elf. He is super-confident and giggles all the time when he's on stage, so he misses some of his lines. I think he got the part because he's Mrs. Sinclair's nephew. She won't yell at him, so the rest of us have to. But he doesn't listen to anyone. He just jumps around until it's his turn to go on stage. Often, he's so busy jumping that he misses his cue and barges on stage at the wrong time.

5. I think the set and the music are some of the best things about our play. We are having a string quartet coming in to play for us. They are excellent. One of them is my cello teacher! They played the music for our production last year, and they sold a lot of their CDs to the audience members afterwards.

6. The set has been made by the senior art class at the local high school, and I think it's perfect. Everyone who has seen it stops and stares in amazement. How they used chicken wire, paper, and paint to make such a realistic and spooky-looking forest, I really don't know. I am terrible at arts and crafts.

7. I had better go to the dress rehearsal now. Wish me luck!

—Ella

Name _____

Use the strategies you learned and practiced in *Lost!* to help you make predictions.

> **Remember:**
> - You need to find and underline the information related to each question.
> - The answer is not in the text, but there is information you can use and think about.
> - The writer will suggest, rather than tell, what is likely to happen.
> - Check all possible answers before making a decision.

1. If Ella were to participate in the theater group's next production, what would she be least likely to do?

   (a) act

   (b) help make the set design

   (c) help with the music

   (d) help Mrs. Sinclair

> **Think!**
> Read Ella's comments on each of these things to find out which one she dislikes or is the least talented at.

2. Which of these things is most likely to happen if Ella goes blank on stage?

   (a) She will run offstage.

   (b) The other cast members will laugh at her.

   (c) She will make up lines on the spot.

   (d) She will laugh about it.

3. What kind of costume do you think Ella will end up wearing? Give reasons for your answer.

   _____

   _____

   _____

4. If something were to go wrong on the opening night of the play, which of these things is it most likely to be?

   (a) The musicians will forget their music.

   (b) Ella's costume won't fit her.

   (c) Mr. Johns will refuse to go on stage.

   (d) The audience will laugh at the set.

5. Do you think Jeremy will completely spoil the play on opening night? Explain why/why not.

   _____

   _____

   _____

Name _____

Activity: Read the story below, and use pages 58–60 to show how well you can sequence, find similarities and differences, and predict.

Terrible Twins' Tale to Hit Big Screen

1. American director Brock Coleson announced in an interview yesterday that he is going to make a movie based on the true story of Belinda and Isabel Kidd.

2. Born in 1970 in a small town in New Zealand, Belinda and Isabel were labeled as "geniuses" by their teachers. Belinda had a particular interest in and talent for art, while Isabel concentrated on mathematics and history. Isabel then went on to study art history and archaeology at a university, while Belinda did courses in makeup artistry and painting, excelling at both. She was also able to sell many of her paintings. According to their few friends, both girls were described as "shy" and "the sort of girls who kept to themselves." The twins were not identical, and apart from their red hair, they did not even look like sisters.

3. After Isabel finished her college degree, the girls decided to go to Europe, using the money they had saved from their part-time jobs in fast food and Belinda's earnings from selling her artwork. The trip was supposed to last six weeks. But it was not to be. A few weeks into their vacation, much to their family and friends' surprise, the Kidds were appearing in European newspapers. The twins claimed that while vacationing in France, they had found two paintings by famous artists that had never been seen before. The art world was amazed and curious. The paintings were inspected by a renowned art expert and declared to be genuine. Promptly, they were sold for millions of dollars at auction. The girls then seemed to disappear. Over the next six months, their parents back in New Zealand received occasional letters from Isabel saying that she and Belinda were well and happy and continuing with their travels. They had rejected the offer of interviews from the media, as they both "didn't want to be famous," she said.

4. But the truth was about to come out. The paintings were examined again by another art expert, and to the new owner's horror, they were found to be clever fakes. Investigation by police revealed that the first art expert had been in on the twins' hoax. In return for declaring the paintings to be real, the twins had promised him half the money they made. But they had vanished too quickly, and he had never been able to claim his money. He said that he had met only Belinda in person when she had turned up at his London office and explained their plan. He said he didn't have a clue where the twins were now.

5. Police are still hunting for the twins to this day. Family and friends claim they have had no contact with them.

6. In the meantime, Coleson has great plans for his movie. "The movie will be based on some of the events in the Kidds' lives," he said in the interview. "Other events will be fictionalized to make the story more exciting. One interesting fact that I will take into account is that I believe the twins' parents received a letter just a few weeks ago that seemed to be in Isabel's handwriting. It said that she and Belinda were sorry for what they had done and were planning to make amends for their crime. However, the parents have denied the letter exists." Coleson would not say who the target audience for his movie is but said he was hoping to attract a "younger" audience.

Name _____

> ### Remember:
>
> - Make sure you know which events you need to sequence, then find and underline them.
> - Determine how they are related. Look for time-marker words.
> - Check all possible answers before making a decision.

1. What did Isabel and Belinda do after Isabel finished her degree?

(a) They saved up their money.

(b) They went to a small town in New Zealand.

(c) They went to Europe.

(d) They sold some of Belinda's paintings.

2. In order, list three things that happened in between the two events below.

• The two paintings were inspected by the first art expert and declared to be genuine.

• _____

• _____

• _____

• The paintings were inspected by the second art expert.

3. What happened a few weeks into Isabel and Belinda's vacation?

(a) The police began hunting for them.

(b) They went to France.

(c) They were labeled as "geniuses."

(d) They appeared in European newspapers.

4. Write the numbers 1 to 4 to place these events in the order in which they happened in "real life."

☐ Coleson announced he was going to make a movie based on the Kidds' lives.

☐ Isabel wrote that she and Belinda didn't want to be famous.

☐ The paintings were found to be clever fakes.

☐ Belinda did a course in makeup artistry.

Finding Similarities and Differences

Name _____

> **Remember:**
> - Make sure you understand the question and underline the keywords.
> - Use a chart or Venn diagram if you need to.
> - Check all possible answers before making a decision.

1. Which of these two things did the twins have in common?

   (a) excellent at painting and red-haired

   (b) interested in mathematics and excellent at painting

   (c) red-haired and shy

   (d) shy and interested in mathematics

2. Isabel and Belinda are different because:

   (a) only Belinda did a course in art history.

   (b) only Isabel kept to herself at school.

   (c) only Belinda met the first art expert.

   (d) only Isabel is being hunted by the police.

3. Explain the difference between the first and second art experts.

   _____

   _____

   _____

   _____

4. Use the Venn diagram to help you to answer the questions below.

   Belinda — Did painting courses, Sold her paintings | red hair, shy, genius | **Isabel** — Wrote to parents, Studied art history

   (a) Who was shy and sold her paintings? _____

   (b) Who studied art history and had red hair? _____

   (c) Who was a genius and shy? _____

   (d) Who had red hair and did a painting course? _____

Name _____

> ### Remember:
> - You need to find and underline the information related to each question.
> - The answer is not in the text, but there is information you can use and think about.
> - The writer will suggest, rather than tell, what is likely to happen.
> - Check all possible answers before making a decision.

1. If the first art expert were to find the twins, which of these things would he be most likely to do?

   (a) turn them into the police

   (b) tell them about the movie

   (c) pay them money

   (d) plan another art hoax with them

2. Do you think the twins will try another art hoax? Explain why/why not.

   _____

   _____

   _____

   _____

3. Write how you think Belinda and Isabel would react to the news of the movie being made. Give reasons.

   _____

   _____

   _____

   _____

4. Most likely, which of these scenes would Coleson most want in his movie?

   (a) Belinda and Isabel eating lunch

   (b) the police chasing and very nearly catching the twins

   (c) Belinda selling her paintings

   (d) the twins working in their classroom at school

Drawing Conclusions

Lesson Objective

- Students will make judgments and reach conclusions based on facts and/or details provided in a text.

Background Information

This section demonstrates how to decide on the meaning of facts and details provided in a text and how to build up evidence in order to make judgments and reach conclusions about the information.

Students also need to be able to search for evidence to support a particular conclusion by locating the relevant information in the text and then making judgments about it.

In higher-order comprehension skills such as this, answers are not always immediately obvious, and discussion about why one answer is judged to be the best should be encouraged. However, teachers may decide to accept another answer if a student can provide the necessary evidence to support the answer he or she has given.

Activity Answers

The Mystery of *Mary Celeste* ....**Pages 65–68**

- Practice Page: Page 67
    1. (d)　　　　2. (c)
    3. Answers may include: They were sailing ships. They were quite large. They required navigation equipment and a compass to sail. They carried cargo. They required a crew. They traveled long distances, etc.
    4. Possible answers: No useful information was ever found. The whereabouts of the people on board was unknown. People often construct rumors out of nothing.
    5. Answers will vary for (a) and (b).

- On Your Own: Page 68
    1. (c)　　　　2. (c)
    3. It had been in the ocean for over one hundred years, and nothing was discovered the first time there was an investigation.
    4. Answers will vary for (a) and (b). Possible answer: People taken by UFOs.
    5. Answers will vary for (a) and (b). Possible answer: Probably not due to the amount of time that has passed and lack of records.

The Castle Tour ....**Pages 69–70**

- Try It Out: Page 70
    1. (c)　　　　2. (d)
    3. Answers will vary for (a) and (b). Possible answer: No, as he was looking at a group of tourists and said that no one was down there.
    4. Possible answer: The information about the implements graphically detailed how they were used to torture people.
    5. Possible answers:
        (a) She was curious about it and thought it would be "cool."
        (b) She felt frightened and panicked about being locked in because she screamed for help, shuddered, and banged on the door.
    6. Answers will vary. Possible answers: She felt panicked; her heart began to pound.

Assessment Answers

Drawing Conclusions ....**Page 84**

    1. (d)　　　　2. (b)
    3. Answers will vary. Possible answers: Her husband is involved; the cave is under her house; there were formal dresses and makeup found in the cave.
    4. They were hiding it from family members, the cave is so well hidden, Uncle Pete tells Isaac that things are going to be very different now that he knows their secret.
    5. Answers will vary for (a) and (b).

Lesson Objective

- Students will summarize text by linking important information and identifying the main points.

Background Information

To be able to summarize text successfully, students first need to be clear about what they are being asked to do and what form their answer should take. (For example, a one-word answer or a more detailed explanation may be required.) It will help if they underline the keywords in the question.

They then need to locate any relevant information in the text, underline it, and establish how it is linked. Words such as *while, but, and, when,* and *as* may be significant in establishing how the information is linked. Unnecessary and irrelevant information should be omitted and the main points established for inclusion in the summary.

Students may need to locate information throughout the entire text in order to summarize the main points for some questions.

Answers may vary and will require teacher review. Those given below are provided as a guide to the main points.

Activity Answers

Wolfgang Amadeus Mozart..**Pages 71–74**

- Practice Page: Page 73
  1. (d)   2. (c)
  3. Jupiter Symphony; Operas - *The Marriage of Figaro, Don Giovanni, The Magic Flute.*
  4. He played different instruments, displaying amazing talent at a very early age, and wrote his first composition at the age of six.
  5. Paragraph should include some or all of the following: Lived in Vienna; married Constanze Weber; six children; freelance musician and a music teacher; spent money unwisely; died in 1791 at 35 years old and was buried in an unmarked grave.

- On Your Own: Page 74
  1. (c)   2. (d)
  3. Mozart and the archbishop of Salzburg often argued.
  4. Possible answers: Childhood musical genius; wrote first composition at six; wrote first symphony at eight and first opera at 12; talented musician and composed historic classical pieces still popular today.
  5. Possible answers: His father taught him and recognized his talent; took him on tour; tried to persuade him not to marry.

Reality TV... **Pages 75–76**

- Try It Out: Page 76
  1. (d)   2. (c)
  3. It is taking jobs away from unemployed actors, causing the number of dramatic and comedy shows on television to decline.
  4. Not educational or entertaining; actors unable to get jobs; people should model responsible behavior; not even reality as actors sometimes used.
  5. (a) The shows do not model good values or how to treat others.
     (b) Answers will vary.

Assessment Answers

Summarizing ....**Page 85**
  1. (c)   2. (b)
  3. Waited five minutes; went into the bedroom; checked in the wardrobe, under the bed, and in the chest of drawers; looked behind the paintings; spoke aloud.
  4. Isaac discovered a large cupboard and a bookshelf containing many books covered in cardboard with pages filled with shapes and patterns.
  5. Isaac found different costumes in the wardrobe such as military clothes, dresses, and suits. He also found boxes of wigs, makeup, and fake noses.

Lesson Objective

- Students will make inferences about what is most likely to be true based on information provided in the text.

Background Information

Inferences are opinions about what is most likely to be true and are formed after careful evaluation of all the available information. Students need to realize that because there is no information that tells them the actual answer, their inferences may not be correct. They have to determine what makes the most sense given the information provided and to then look for details to support their decisions. They may need to use some prior knowledge to help them determine their answer.

The focus of this section is on teaching students how to use contextual information, both written and visual, to determine what they believe to be true. They then must find further evidence to support their decisions.

Student answers will need to be checked by the teacher, but some possible answers have been provided as a guide.

Activity Answers

Ballet on a Board .... **Pages 77–80**

- Practice Page: Page 79
  1. (b)
  2. Answers may include: (a) Dancing felt unnatural and uncomfortable. It was hard work. Lessons were stressful and seemed like a punishment.
     (b) Surfing felt free and natural. She felt at home and exhilarated.
  3. (a) Thomas Blair believes that people will think better of him and his wife if Kerry dances well.
     (b) Emily Blair thinks that Kerry will benefit from ballet now and in the future.
  4. Advantages—body strength, fitness, flexibility, discipline, posture, grace, poise
     Disadvantages—hard work, long hours, no fun, no time for other activities
- On Your Own: Page 80
  1. (c)   2. Answers will vary for (a) and (b).
  3. Possible answer: Probably yes, because she'll realize ballet helped her surf well.
  4. Answers may include: (a) active, energetic, pleasant, sociable
     (b) good, because she continued to do ballet and thinks they'll let her pursue surfing
  5. Answers will vary for (a) and (b).

To Be Sold by Auction .... **Pages 81–82**

- Try It Out: Page 82
  1. (d)   2. (a)
  3. His wife had died, but he felt she was still with him.
  4. Possible answer: He was feeling sad, but he smiled as he remembered all the happy things that had happened in the house.
  5. The slamming door interrupted his daydreams about the past, and he just saw the house as it really was and he left.
  6. Possible answers: (a) happy
     (b) happy children, laughing children, happily working together, lovingly watched over, beaming smile, beloved and always smiling, with pleasure, welcoming embrace, squeals of mischievous laughter, peaceful dreams.

Assessment Answers

Making Inferences ....**Page 86**

1. (d)   2. (b)
3. He was surprised when he realized that his uncle and aunt wore disguises.
4. Answers will vary. Possible answer: They could be secret agents working for the government.
5. Answers will vary for (a) and (b). Possible answer: Isaac won't be allowed to go home so that their secret would be safe.
6. Possible answer: He thought his aunt and uncle's secret was an evil one, and he had to inform others about it.

DRAWING CONCLUSIONS

- Make sure you understand what it is you are drawing conclusions about.
- Look in the text to find the facts and details.
- Make decisions about what they mean.
- Always check all possible answers before deciding on your answer.

SUMMARIZING

- Check the text to be sure you understand the question. Then, find the keywords.
- Find information in the text that is most important to your understanding of it. Decide how it is connected.
- Take out any unnecessary details or unconnected information.
- Always check all possible answers before deciding on your answer.

MAKING INFERENCES

- The answers are usually not in the text, but there is information that will give you clues to think about.
- Find the answer that makes the most sense and is supported by the text.
- Always consider all possible answers before making a decision.

Drawing Conclusions

Name _____

Conclusions are decisions or judgments we make after considering all the information. We draw conclusions about what we read by finding facts and details in the text, taking it all into consideration, and then making judgments about it.

Activity: Read the passage below and complete pages 66–68.

The Mystery of Mary Celeste

1. On November 7, 1872, a 100-foot sailing ship called *Mary Celeste* left from New York Harbor on a voyage to Genoa, Italy—a destination she would never reach. The ship was carrying a cargo of 1,700 barrels of raw industrial alcohol. On board were Captain Benjamin Briggs, a well-regarded and experienced sea captain; his wife, Sarah; their two-year-old daughter, Sophia; and a crew of seven.

2. A week later, another cargo ship called *Dei Gratia* also left on a voyage from New York Harbor, following a similar course across the Atlantic. On December 5, *Dei Gratia*'s crew sighted *Mary Celeste* in the Bay of Gibraltar near the Portuguese coastline and decided that she was drifting, although no distress signals could be seen. Some of the crew launched a small boat and rowed to *Mary Celeste*. When they boarded the ship, they discovered that, although *Mary Celeste* was a "wet mess," she was in seaworthy condition. But no one was on board. All 10 people had vanished without a trace.

3. The crew searched the ship and found that the cargo and the food and water supply were still there. However, the lifeboat and the navigation instruments were missing. It appeared as if the people on board *Mary Celeste* had left in a hurry. The *Dei Gratia* crew eventually sailed *Mary Celeste* to Gibraltar and a court of investigation examined the ship but failed to come up with a definite answer to the puzzle. *Mary Celeste* was then sailed by a number of different owners for another 12 years before it was wrecked and sank off the coast of Haiti.

4. Over the years, many stories and rumors about what was found on *Mary Celeste* have been circulated. Some people say there was a bloody sword under Captain Briggs's bed, that there were scratches and bloodstains along one of the ship's railings, that the only compass had been destroyed, and that the ship's cat had been discovered aboard, fast asleep!

5. In addition, many theories linger as to what happened to the people on board. Some of these theories are more likely than others. Did the crew try to escape in the lifeboat because Captain Briggs thought the ship was sinking or because the cargo of alcohol began exploding? Did a UFO land and kidnap the people on board? Did pirates attack the ship? Did the ship collide with a giant squid? Did the crew murder Captain Briggs and his family and then escape? We may never know.

6. The wreck of *Mary Celeste* was discovered in 2001, but experts believe that it is unlikely to provide any new information about the fate of the people on board. For the moment, the story of *Mary Celeste* remains one of the great mysteries of the ocean.

Name _____

Follow the steps below to learn how to draw conclusions.

> - Conclusions are decisions or judgments you make after careful consideration of facts and details in the text.
> - Make sure you understand what it is you are drawing conclusions about.
> - Look in the text to find the facts and details and underline them.
> - You will need to make decisions about what they mean.
> - Always check all possible answers before making a decision.

1. You can conclude the people on board *Mary Celeste* left in a hurry because:

(a) Captain Briggs was a very experienced sailor.

(b) they were near the Portuguese coastline.

(c) the ship was discovered drifting.

(d) the food and water supplies were left on board.

2. Choose the best answer. Think about each choice carefully.

(a) This statement is true but does not relate to why they left in a hurry. This is not the best answer.

(b) They were near the Portuguese coastline, but this information also doesn't relate to why they left in a hurry. This is not the best answer.

(c) The fact that the ship was drifting indicates that there was no one on board, but it doesn't relate to the people leaving in a hurry. This is not a good answer.

(d) It would be important for the crew to take food and water supplies with them if they abandoned the ship, but they didn't, which probably means they left in a hurry. This is the best answer.

1. Because the navigation instruments and lifeboat were discovered missing, you can conclude that:

(a) the pirates stole them.

(b) the captain and crew abandoned the ship.

(c) the captain had become lost.

(d) the ship had been severely damaged.

2. Choose the best answer. Think about each choice carefully.

(a) If pirates had boarded the ship, then it could be assumed that the cargo would also be missing, but it was found on board the ship. This is probably not the best answer.

(b) If the passengers on board *Mary Celeste* had abandoned the ship, they would have taken the lifeboat and navigation instruments. This is so far the best answer, but remember to read all the possible answers.

(c) As the Captain was very experienced, it is unlikely he had become lost. This is not the best answer.

(d) The text mentioned that the ship was seaworthy and sailed for another 12 years, so it could not have been severely damaged. This is not the best answer.

Drawing Conclusions

Name _____

Use the strategies you learned to practice drawing conclusions. Use the clues in the "Think!" boxes to help you.

1. You can conclude that the theory about *Mary Celeste* colliding with a giant squid is most likely untrue because:
   (a) giant squids don't exist.
   (b) colliding with a giant squid would do little damage to a sailing ship.
   (c) the experienced Captain could have avoided the squid.
   (d) the ship was found to be in good condition.

> **Think!**
> Read paragraph 2 to help you justify the conclusion.

2. The *Dei Gratia* crew concluded that they should board *Mary Celeste* because:
   (a) they saw a distress signal.
   (b) they wanted to see who was on board.
   (c) they decided that she was drifting.
   (d) they could see she was a wet mess.

> **Think!**
> Read paragraph 2.

3. Write two pieces of information you can conclude about ships in the 1870s.
   - _____
     _____
   - _____
     _____

> **Think!**
> Read the first three paragraphs, and underline any information relating to ships to help you to draw conclusions.

4. Why do you think the information about what was found on board *Mary Celeste* (bloody sword, cat, etc.) are only stories and rumors, not facts?

   _____
   _____
   _____

> **Think!**
> Read paragraph 4 and think about what is known about the mystery surrounding *Mary Celeste* to help you draw a conclusion.

5. (a) Which theory about the disappearance of the people on board *Mary Celeste* do you think is the most likely to be true?

   _____

   (b) Explain why you reached this conclusion.

   _____
   _____
   _____

> **Think!**
> Read each theory again to help you make a conclusion about which one is most likely true.

Name _____

Use the strategies you have been practicing to help you draw conclusions.

1. You can conclude the theory about pirates attacking the ship is unlikely because:

    (a) pirates are known to be the friendly people of the sea.

    (b) there was not a pirate flag flying on board *Mary Celeste*.

    (c) the valuable cargo was still on board the ship.

    (d) the ship was found in good condition.

2. How was the crew of the second ship most likely feeling as they climbed on board the drifting *Mary Celeste*?

    (a) annoyed that they had to leave their own ship

    (b) frightened of the sharks in the water below

    (c) uneasy about what they might find on the ship

    (d) excited that they had made the discovery

3. You can conclude the reason why experts don't believe they will find any new information from the wreck of *Mary Celeste* found in 2001 is because . . .

    _____

    _____

    _____

4. (a) Which theory given about the disappearance of the people on board *Mary Celeste* do you think is the least likely to be true?

    _____

    (b) Explain why you reached this conclusion. _____

    _____

    _____

    _____

5. (a) Do you think the truth about the disappearance of the people on board *Mary Celeste* will ever be discovered?

    ☐ Yes   ☐ No

    (b) Explain why you reached this conclusion. _____

    _____

    _____

    _____

Drawing Conclusions

Name _____

Activity: Read the story below and complete page 70.

The Castle Tour

1. "Please follow me." The tour guide hoisted her umbrella in the air and strode off. I rolled my eyes and began to shuffle after her until I felt Dad's hand on my shoulder.

2. "Wait, Jasmine. Mom's just…" Dad pointed towards the gift shop we had just passed.

3. I nodded wearily. "I'll wait here for you." I leaned against the crumbling wall and closed my eyes, feeling the sun's warmth. I didn't really care about the tour anyway. It was fun to be wandering around a castle, but the tour guide was snappy and had an irritating voice.

4. "Come on, young lady, move along please. Everyone's waiting for you." I opened my eyes to see the tour guide glaring at me.

5. "But I'm just…"

6. "You can't stay here on your own. Let's go." She grasped my elbow and began to march me towards the group, who were looking at their watches and clicking their tongues. "It's all right, everyone. I found her."

7. I struggled from her grip. "I'm waiting…"

8. But by now she had begun talking into her microphone. It boomed around the courtyard we had entered. She had positioned me right in front of her. I glanced back anxiously towards the shop. Mom and Dad were nowhere to be seen, so they still had to be inside. I waited until the tour guide turned her head to show the group the castle walls behind her, then I tiptoed back towards the shop.

9. But I never got there. A sign to my right caught my eye. "Torture Chamber," I read. Cool! The tour guide hadn't mentioned that. I paused and looked at my watch. The castle was about to close in 10 minutes. Mom always took ages in stores—she'd easily be in the gift shop for at least that long. If I went and asked if we could look in the torture chamber, she and Dad might say no. So…

10. I hesitated for just one more moment, then headed towards the sign. It would take only a minute to have just a quick look. The bored-looking guard who was standing at the entrance was focused on a group of tourists as I slipped past him and trudged down the dark stairs. It was silent and smelled musty. When I reached the bottom, only faint lights were glowing. It was a small room with all sorts of horrible-looking implements made of wood and iron in display cabinets. I read the descriptions of some of them and shivered. This wasn't a nice place to be on your own. I decided to head back into the sunlight to find Mom and Dad. As I started towards the stairs, I heard voices above.

11. "All clear, Harry?"

12. "Yep. I just checked a few minutes ago. No one's down there."

13. "We'll close it now, then. Help me with the door, will you?"

14. My heart began to pound, and I raced up the stairs. "No!" I yelled.

15. But it was too late. The iron door clanged into place, plunging the stairs into total darkness.

16. "Help me!" I screamed. "I'm still in here!"

17. Silence answered me. I shuddered and banged on the door with my fists. "Please let me out!"

18. I continued to scream for several minutes. Eventually, my throat on fire, I sank to the ground. I didn't know how long it would take until someone found me, but I knew I wasn't going to enjoy the wait.

Name _____

Use the strategies you learned and practiced in *The Mystery of* Mary Celeste to help you with drawing conclusions.

> **Remember:**
> - Make sure you understand the question and what you are drawing conclusions about.
> - Look in the text for facts and details and underline them.
> - Decide what they mean.
> - Check all possible answers before making a decision.

1. You can conclude that the people on the tour were looking at their watches because:

   (a) they were hungry and wanted their dinner.

   (b) they thought the tour was taking far too long.

   (c) they had to wait for Jasmine to be found for the tour to continue.

   (d) they were in a hurry to get to the torture chamber.

> **Think!**
> Read paragraph 6.

2. You can conclude Jasmine was desperate to get out of the torture chamber because:

   (a) she was worried her parents would leave without her.

   (b) she was afraid of the dark.

   (c) her hands and her throat were hurting.

   (d) she was in a dark and terribly scary place.

3. (a) Do you think the guard saw Jasmine enter the torture chamber? ☐ Yes ☐ No

   (b) Explain why you reached this conclusion.

   _____

   _____

4. What can you conclude about the descriptions Jasmine read of some of the implements in the torture chamber?

   _____

   _____

5. Why could you conclude that Jasmine...

   (a) wanted to go into the torture chamber? _____

   _____

   (b) wanted to leave again after only a short time? _____

   _____

6. How do you think Jasmine felt when she heard the iron door clang into place? Base your conclusion on information provided in the text.

   _____

Summarizing

Name _____

Summarizing is giving the main ideas and facts without using many words. We need to link the important ideas and decide which are the main points.

Activity: Read the passage below and complete pages 72–74.

Wolfgang Amadeus Mozart

1. Wolfgang Amadeus Mozart was a famous composer of classical music and is considered to be one of the greatest musical geniuses of all time. Although he died at the age of 35, he wrote more than 600 musical compositions.

2. Mozart was born on January 27, 1756, in Salzburg, Austria. His father, Leopold, was well known throughout Europe as a music teacher, and he was also a successful composer. Around the age of three, Mozart learned to play the harpsichord (a keyboard instrument that preceded the piano), showing an amazing musical talent. His father also taught him to play the violin and the organ. Mozart wrote his first two compositions when he was just six years old.

3. When Mozart turned seven, his father decided to take him and his sister, Nannerl, on a tour of the royal courts of Europe to show off their musical abilities. Nannerl was a talented harpsichord player, although she did not show the same genius for music as her brother. The children played all over Europe until Mozart was in his late teens, making Leopold a large sum of money and building Mozart's reputation as a musician. During these tours, Mozart met not only kings and queens but also many famous musicians and composers, learning a great deal more about music and composing. Mozart was also busy writing music. He composed his first symphony at the age of eight and his first opera at the age of 12! He composed other works for orchestras as well as pieces for the harpsichord, violin, and other instruments, many of which were performed publicly.

4. In 1769 (at age 13), Mozart began working for the archbishop of Salzburg as the "concertmaster" of the Salzburg Court Orchestra. He did not get along well with the archbishop, and the two often argued. Part of the reason for this was because Mozart was away from Salzburg on tour so often. Mozart eventually left this position (most people agree he was probably dismissed by the archbishop) in 1781.

5. In 1782, now living in Vienna, Mozart married Constanze Weber against his father's wishes. The couple would later have six children, but only two would reach adulthood. Mozart now earned a living as a freelance musician—he sold his compositions, performed, and worked as a music teacher. He earned what was regarded as a good income for a musician; however, he spent his money unwisely and often had to borrow from his friends to support his family.

6. Mozart died in Vienna on December 5, 1791 from an unknown illness. He was buried in an unmarked grave as was the custom of the time for many funerals and burials. Mozart's music remains popular with musicians and music lovers around the world and includes the *Jupiter Symphony* and the operas *The Marriage of Figaro, Don Giovanni,* and *The Magic Flute.*

Learning Page

Name _____

Follow the steps below and learn how to identify the main points and summarize text.

- Make sure you understand the question and underline keywords.
- Look for information in the text, and decide what is important and how it is connected.
- Omit any unnecessary or unconnected information.
- Always check all possible answers before making a decision.

1. Which sentence would best be left out of a summary about Mozart's childhood?

   (a) He was born in Salzburg, Austria.

   (b) At a young age, he was already a very talented musician and composer.

   (c) He composed his first opera at the age of 12.

   (d) He married against his father's wishes.

2. Choose the best answer. Think about each choice carefully.

   (a) Where Mozart was born is an important fact and should be in the summary. This is not the best answer.

   (b) The fact that Mozart was talented at such an early age is an important statement and should be included. This is not best the answer.

   (c) The age Mozart composed his first opera should also be in the summary. This is not the best answer.

   (d) This fact is about Mozart when he was an adult and should not be in the summary of his childhood. This is the best answer.

1. Which sentence best summarizes why Mozart's sister, Nannerl, did not achieve the same extraordinary fame as her brother?

   (a) She had no musical abilities.

   (b) Her father was not interested in her musical performances.

   (c) She was not as musically gifted as her brother.

   (d) She was able to play only the harpsichord.

2. Choose the best answer. Think about each choice carefully.

   (a) Nannerl was a talented harpsichord player, so this is not the best answer.

   (b) Their father took both children on tour to display their musical talent. This is not the best answer.

   (c) The text states that she did not show the musical genius of her brother. This is so far the best answer, but remember to read all the choices first.

   (d) Nannerl could play only the harpsichord, but it does not explain why she didn't achieve similar fame like her brother. This is not the best answer.

Summarizing

Name _____

Use the strategies you learned to practice summarizing. Use the clues in the "Think!" boxes to help you.

1. Which phrase best summarizes Mozart's relationship with the archbishop of Salzburg?

(a) short and peaceful

(b) short and indifferent

(c) long and harmonious

(d) long and hostile

> **Think!**
> Find the text that relates to this part of Mozart's life and read it carefully.

2. Which sentence best summarizes why Mozart was buried in an unmarked grave?

(a) It was all he could afford.

(b) It was all his father would pay for.

(c) Marked gravestones weren't popular at the time.

(d) No one wanted Mozart's fans to know where he was buried.

> **Think!**
> Read paragraph 6 carefully to help you choose an answer to this question.

3. Create a list to summarize Mozart's well-known music compositions.

- _____
- _____
- _____
- _____

> **Think!**
> Read paragraph 6, and underline the important facts.

4. Write a sentence that summarizes how Mozart's musical abilities were first discovered.

_____

_____

_____

_____

> **Think!**
> Paragraph 2 will help you find the information. Only include the important facts.

5. Write a short paragraph that summarizes Mozart's life after 1782.

_____

_____

_____

_____

_____

> **Think!**
> Find the section of the text that relates to this question, and underline the important facts for your summary.

Name _____

Use the strategies you have been practicing to help you summarize text.

1. Which sentence would best be left out of a summary about Mozart's childhood?

(a) At eight years old, he composed his first symphony.

(b) Mozart performed for kings and queens across Europe.

(c) He taught music to support his family.

(d) He toured Europe with his father and sister.

2. Which sentence best summarizes why Mozart was forced to borrow money from his friends?

(a) The cost of living was extremely high in the 1780s.

(b) Mozart's family was extremely careless with money.

(c) Mozart's earned little as a music teacher.

(d) Mozart lacked judgment when it came to his finances.

3. Write a sentence to summarize the reasons why Mozart was no longer the concertmaster of the Salzburg Court Orchestra as of 1781.

_____

_____

_____

4. Choose facts from the text you would use to summarize why Mozart is considered to be one of the greatest musical geniuses of all time.

- _____

- _____

- _____

- _____

5. Write a summary explaining how Mozart's father influenced, or tried to influence, his son's life.

_____

_____

_____

_____

_____

_____

Name _____

Activity: Read the story below and complete page 76.

Reality TV

To whom it may concern,

1.   This letter is to express my concern regarding the quality of the shows your network has chosen to broadcast lately. I have been a loyal viewer of your station for quite some time, but recently I have been disappointed with your selection of shows—more specifically, your wide array of reality television shows. I am aware that reality television has become quite popular in the last five years, and people I know watch at least one or two of them a week. But, I think reality television is a waste of time and should be replaced with quality shows that are worthy of our viewing time.

2.   First, I prefer television shows that provide us with quality education or entertainment experiences—and reality television serves neither of these purposes. You are simply watching ordinary people live out their ordinary lives or deal with ridiculous or unrealistic circumstances. It is "easy-to-watch" television. You don't have to think about much.

3.   Reality television has caused the number of drama and comedy shows produced to decrease, dramatically reducing work opportunities for our country's actors. It would be difficult enough to find work as an entertainer without having to compete with these reality shows. It would be great to watch some interesting drama or comedy series again.

4.   I also think that reality shows generate the wrong role models for society. As many reality shows are watched by young people, I think that the people on reality shows should at least model responsible behavior. Unfortunately, this is not usually the case. I shudder to think what young people are learning about how to treat others from these shows. Some of the values of reality shows are questionable, such as shows that depict entitled children running the household and speaking disrespectfully to adults. What messages are these shows trying to give?

5.   I feel that many of the "reality" television shows your network produces are not even that. The creators of some of your reality shows have admitted that many are scripted or have been carefully designed to make the participants act in a dramatic way to encourage people to watch the show. Others have actually used actors in some scenes without informing the television viewers. This is misleading, and I think production companies, along with your network, should be ashamed.

6.   I know that people say that if you don't like what's on television, you can always turn the channel or switch it off. This may happen, but I feel that as a loyal viewer of your network, I thought that you should be aware of my concerns. I don't think reality television is entertaining, nor is it a benefit to our society. I really hope you take this all into consideration and replace reality shows with quality entertainment.

From your loyal viewer,

Jake

Name _____

Use the strategies you learned and practiced in *Wolfgang Amadeus Mozart* to help you summarize information.

Remember:

- Make sure you understand the question and underline the keywords.
- Look for information in the text, and decide what is important and how it is connected.
- Omit any unnecessary or unconnected information.
- Always check all possible answers before making a decision.

---

1. Which sentence best summarizes why the writer thinks the network should be ashamed?

  (a) They only cast very attractive people.

  (b) They make the cast do crazy things.

  (c) The fans of the show become out of control.

  (d) They mislead their viewers into thinking the shows are completely unscripted.

2. Which sentence best summarizes the writer's purpose for writing this letter?

  (a) to become a cast member on a reality TV show

  (b) to let the network know that he's no longer going to watch their shows

  (c) to encourage the network to replace reality shows with quality entertainment

  (d) to help unemployed actors find jobs

3. Write a sentence to summarize how the writer thinks reality television is destroying opportunities for actors.

  _____

  _____

4. Make a summary of the writer's four main reasons for disliking reality television.

  • _____

  • _____

  • _____

  • _____

Think!

Read the text again, and underline the main reasons the writer states for disliking reality TV and list them (in your own words).

---

5. (a) Write a sentence that summarizes the writer's opinion about reality television and young people.

  _____

  _____

  (b) Write a sentence that summarizes your opinion of reality television.

  _____

  _____

Making Inferences

Name _____

When we read, we often make decisions about what we think is most likely to be true based on the information given in the text. This is called *making inferences*.

Activity: Read the story below and complete pages 78–80.

Ballet on a Board

1. "Saturday morning again!" groaned Kerry as she buried her head under the pillow and began her muffled "I hate ballet" chant. She thought longingly of her friends who would be preparing for a day at the beach, swimming, surfing, and generally having a great time.

2. For as long as she could remember, 13-year-old Kerry Blair had been attending ballet classes. As the only child of Thomas and Emily Blair, former dancers with the National Ballet Company, it was assumed that she would want to follow in her parents' graceful footsteps.

3. Dressed in a leotard and tights, Kerry posed in front of the full-length mirror, imagining she was riding the waves on the surfboard she did not possess. "Oh, why do I have to dance?" she wailed. "I want to wear neoprene, not spandex!"

4. Kerry's mom watched her daughter from the doorway. "You dance, my darling, to give you grace, poise, and a strong body. You will appreciate its value one day. Hurry, your dad's waiting!"

5. "Are you ready, Kerry?" called her father impatiently from the hallway. "It's the final rehearsal today. I want everything to be perfect for the concert. It wouldn't look good if our own daughter let us down, now would it?"

6. After three torturous hours at the studio, Kerry was allowed to join her friends at the beach. As she ran along the sand, she felt like an animal released into its natural habitat after being caged in an unfamiliar environment.

7. "Let me use your board, Clare," Kerry asked her friend. "I need the ocean's healing power to de-stress my danced-out body!"

8. Jumping over the breakers as she entered the water, Kerry was unaware of the two pairs of eyes watching her closely.

9. In the ocean, she felt at home. The surfboard was like an extension of her body. She knew instinctively how to move on the board as it responded to the motion of the wind and waves. One after the other, the waves came and were mastered by the young girl on the borrowed board.

10. As she returned to the beach, exhilarated and exhausted, Kerry was approached by a man and a woman, each wearing the official jackets of a famous surfing company. They introduced themselves, explaining that they were scouting for new surfing talent to prepare for surfing competitions in forthcoming years.

11. Kerry was speechless. "Me? But I don't even own a board! I've only been surfing for one season. How can you possibly be asking me?"

12. "You have such poise and elegance on the board," enthused the woman. "With the great strength you demonstrate, I'd say you are a naturally gifted surfer. You have the potential to go a long way in the sport. Are you interested?"

13. "Interested?" squealed Kerry. "You wait until I tell my folks! Dad will take a bit of convincing, but Mom will be a pushover!"

Name _____

Follow the steps below to learn how to determine what is most likely to be true.

- The answers are not usually in the text, but there is information given that will give you clues to think about. (This could be underlined.)
- Find the answer that makes the most sense and is supported by text details.
- Always consider all possible answers before making a decision.

1. What is the best reason why Kerry said she hated ballet?

(a) She was not very good at it.

(b) She wanted to stay in bed on Saturday mornings.

(c) Her parents forced her to dance because they were dancers.

(d) She wanted to spend her time surfing instead.

2. Choose the best answer. Think about each choice carefully.

(a) There is nothing in the text to indicate that she wasn't very good at ballet. This is not a good answer.

(b) It is possible that she would have preferred to stay in bed rather than go to ballet, but the text does not imply that she wanted to stay in bed. This is an unlikely answer.

(c) The text does state that Kerry had been dancing for years and that it was assumed she would follow her parents into dancing. It is possible, though not certain, that she was forced to dance. This is a possible answer.

(d) Throughout the text, it is implied that Kerry would rather be surfing than dancing. This is the best answer.

1. What is the best reason why Kerry was such a good surfer?

(a) She had been surfing for as long as she could remember.

(b) She loved surfing so much.

(c) Her ballet training had developed her strength and body management.

(d) She knew how to move on the board.

2. Choose the best answer. Think about each choice carefully.

(a) This is not true. She had been surfing for one season only. This is not a good answer.

(b) Although it is true that she loved surfing, it is not the reason why she was good at it. This is an unlikely answer.

(c) Strength and good body management are essential for good surfing, and she had developed this through ballet. This is a very good answer, but you must read all of them.

(d) This is true; she could move well on a board, but it does not give enough information. This is a possible answer, but (c) is a better answer.

Making Inferences

Name _____

Use the strategies you learned to practice making inferences. Use the clues in the "Think!" boxes to help you.

1. What is the best reason why Kerry's parents wanted her to dance?

    (a) They wanted her to become a famous ballet dancer.

    (b) They wanted to prepare her for whatever activity she may later choose.

    (c) They wanted her to follow the family tradition.

    (d) They assumed she wanted to dance because they had.

> **Think!**
> Read what her mom says in paragraph 4 and what the female official says in paragraph 12.

2. Read paragraphs 6 and 7. How does the writer explain how Kerry felt . . .

    (a) about dancing? _____

    _____

    _____

    (b) about surfing? _____

    _____

    _____

> **Think!**
> Consider how an animal feels when taken from its natural habitat.

3. Why do each of Kerry's parents want her to dance?

    (a) Thomas Blair _____

    _____

    _____

    (b) Emily Blair _____

    _____

    _____

> **Think!**
> Who are Kerry's parents thinking of as they speak? See paragraphs 4 and 5.

4. Write a list of advantages and disadvantages Kerry might write about ballet.

Advantages	Disadvantages

> **Think!**
> - After many years of dancing, what physical benefits would she be aware of?
> - How many times a week do you think she may have to practice?
> - How might this affect her social life?

Name _____

Use the strategies you have been practicing to help you make inferences.

1. What were Kerry's thoughts after being approached by the surfing scouts?

   (a) She was worried that her parents might not be able to afford to pay for her surfing.

   (b) She could not give up dancing because it would upset her parents too much.

   (c) She knew her parents would respect her choice.

   (d) She could split her time between dancing and surfing.

2. How do you think Kerry's news will be received by . . .

   (a) her mother? _____

   _____

   _____

   (b) her father? _____

   _____

   _____

3. Do you think Kerry will change her opinion about dancing? Give reasons for your answer.

   _____

   _____

   _____

4. (a) Describe the sort of person you think Kerry is.

   _____

   _____

   (b) What sort of relationship do you think she has with her parents? Give reasons for your answer.

   _____

   _____

5. Write words/phrases to describe how Kerry felt when she was . . .

   (a) dancing.   (b) surfing.

Making Inferences

Name _____

Activity: Read the story below and complete page 82.

To Be Sold by Auction

1. The elderly gentleman stood across the street, staring at the imposing Victorian house. Despite the neatly clipped bushes and well maintained lawn, it appeared, to him, desolate. After a moment of hesitation, he took a deep breath, crossed the road, and crunched up the gravel drive, not stopping to study the real estate agent's sign. He followed the path that took him through to the backyard.

2. The scene caused his eyes to prickle with unshed tears. As he scanned the view, he saw visions of past seasons; daffodils of early spring giving way to bluebells and poppies as the summer progressed; happy children kicking through piles of leaves recently fallen from trees preparing for the winter; the same laughing children building snowmen and throwing snowballs as the cold air gave their cheeks a rosy glow. He smiled sadly, a lump forming in his throat.

3. In the small orchard, he saw a family happily working together harvesting the golden fruit, a man and his son preparing the soil for next year's vegetable crop, and a toddler planting seeds, lovingly watched over by her adoring mother. The woman looked up and waved, a beaming smile spreading across her face. James and Hannah were grown up now, living abroad with families of their own. And their mother ... she had left him now but would always be with him wherever he was. Was he foolish to come back? Would he always feel this forlorn? The gentleman turned and walked into the house through the back door.

4. It was completely empty, yet it retained hard evidence of previous occupation. There were marks on the walls where photographs, pictures, mirrors, and clocks used to hang and scuff marks on the paintwork from years of assault by footwear, bags, and children's toys. But there was something else that only he could feel.

5. As he walked from room to room, the gentleman closed his eyes. He could see, hear, and smell the secrets of the house's history. In the kitchen was his beloved and always smiling Estelle as she prepared the family meals, the scent of home-baked bread causing him to wrinkle his nose with pleasure. Pushing open the door to the living room, he tensed his body, ready to shield himself from the attack of two small children, throwing themselves at him in a welcoming embrace. He recognized the familiar creaking of the stairs as he climbed towards the bathroom from where squeals of mischievous laughter and soapy perfume were escaping. In a moonlit bedroom, the faces of his peacefully dreaming children brought a smile to his face. As he tiptoed out of the room, a door downstairs slammed in the breeze and the spell was broken.

6. The gentleman shivered though the day was warm. He descended the stairs and left the house by the front door. As he walked down the path, his pace quickened. Without stopping to take a final look, he turned left and marched down the street. The house became, once more, a property to be sold by auction.

Name _____

Use the strategies you learned and practiced in *Ballet on a Board* to help you make inferences.

> ### Remember:
> - The answers are usually not in the text, but there is information given that will give you clues to think about.
> - Find the answer that makes the most sense and is supported by text details.
> - Always consider all possible answers before making a decision.

1. Most likely, what was the connection between the elderly gentleman and the Victorian house?

   (a) He was a prospective buyer.

   (b) The house was his childhood home.

   (c) He used to visit the house as a child.

   (d) He lived in the house with his wife and children.

> ### Think!
> Read through the whole text carefully, paying particular attention to people mentioned.

2. What would be the best reason why the gentleman visited the house?

   (a) He wanted to relive some memories of a happy time.

   (b) He wanted to measure the rooms for furniture, carpets, and curtains.

   (c) He was checking that none of his possessions were left there.

   (d) He was the real estate agent for the sale.

3. Explain the meaning of ". . . she had left him now but would always be with him wherever he was."

   _____

   _____

4. How do you think the gentleman was feeling as he wandered around the property?

   _____

   _____

5. What effect did the door slamming downstairs have on the gentlemen?

   _____

   _____

6. (a) How would you describe the gentleman's memories of the house? _____

   (b) Write a phrase from the text to support your answer.

   _____

   _____

Name _____

Activity: Read the story below, and use pages 84–86 to show how well you can draw conclusions, summarize, and make inferences.

Aunty Belinda and Uncle Pete

1. After I heard the front door slam, I made myself wait five minutes before I dared to enter the room. As soon as the time was up, I leaped to my feet and charged in.

2. I pushed open the door and glanced around the room. There didn't appear to be anything out of the ordinary. But I knew the evidence had to be there somewhere. I checked in the wardrobe, under the bed, and in the chest of drawers. Nothing. Just ordinary things. I even tried searching behind the two paintings on the wall.

3. "Where have you hidden it?" I said aloud. I stomped my foot. "Ow!" I sank to the ground and rubbed my foot. Then, I stopped and stared. There was something sticking up under the floor rug. I pulled it aside. It was a small brass ring attached to a trapdoor in the floorboards.

4. I knew this had to be it! I tugged at the ring, and after a few tries, I managed to pull the trapdoor open. I peered in. All I could see was a staircase, descending into pitch blackness. I was desperate to go down there, but I looked at my watch. If my aunt and uncle had gone to the store, I had about 20 minutes up my sleeve. I hesitated only a moment longer. I put my foot on the first step and began to climb down.

5. After about 10 steps, I could see light softly glowing below. I jumped down the last few steps and found myself in a small rocky cave, lit by a single electric bulb hanging from the ceiling. There was a large cupboard and a bookshelf pushed against one wall. I went to the bookshelf first. All the books looked the same—cardboard covered exercise books. I took one down and flicked it open. The pages were filled with strange shapes and patterns that had been hand-drawn—they looked like codes! The other five I looked at were similar. I shoved the smallest book in my pocket. I was sure it wouldn't be missed in a hurry.

6. Next, I opened the wardrobe and gasped. It was jam-packed with clothes—mostly military uniforms, formal dresses, and mens suits. On the shelf above were five boxes. Four were filled with wigs and beards of all different types, and the fifth contained makeup—lipsticks, powders, eyeliners—there were even some fake noses!

7. I knew now that I wasn't crazy—my aunt and uncle were not all they appeared to be. I had to get back home as soon as possible. I patted my pocket. At least now I had evidence.

8. "Isaac, stay right where you are!" Uncle Pete's voice shattered the silence. My heart began to pound. He was right behind me.

9. "Uncle Pete, I…"

10. "Why did you have to go poking around? You could have gone home tomorrow and continued with your normal life. Now, things are going to be very different."

11. As he spoke, I could see his reflection in the mirror on the inside of the wardrobe door. I could see he wasn't carrying any kind of weapon. I could easily escape past him, but I would have to be quick. I had to get away. It was my duty.

Name _____

Remember:
- Make sure you understand what it is you are drawing conclusions about.
- Look in the text to find the facts and details and underline them.
- Make decisions about what they mean.
- Always check all possible answers before making a decision.

---

1. You can conclude Isaac waited five minutes to enter the room because:

(a) he was watching the end of a television show.

(b) he was nervous about what he would find there.

(c) he was waiting to make sure his aunt and uncle were asleep.

(d) he was waiting to make sure his aunt and uncle were a good distance away.

2. Why do you think Isaac stomped his foot?

(a) He was about to start tap dancing.

(b) He was frustrated he couldn't find any evidence.

(c) He was checking for trapdoors.

(d) His foot was hurting him.

3. You can conclude that Aunty Belinda knows about what is happening because . . .

_____

_____

4. Why can you conclude that Isaac's aunt and uncle are involved in something very secretive?

_____

_____

5. (a) Write two words to describe the type of person you think Isaac is.

_____   _____

(b) Use details from the text to explain why you reached this conclusion.

_____

_____

_____

_____

_____

Name _____

> ## Remember:
> - Make sure you understand the question and underline the keywords.
> - Look for information in the text, and decide what is important and how it is connected.
> - Omit any unnecessary or unconnected information.
> - Always check all possible answers before making a decision.

1. Which sentence best summarizes why Isaac climbed down into the cave?

   (a) He thought his aunt and uncle were in there.

   (b) He had plenty of time and felt like exploring.

   (c) He had just enough time and was very curious to see what was in there.

   (d) He was hoping to find an outfit for a costume party.

2. Which sentence would be best left out of a summary explaining what happened after Uncle Pete spoke?

   (a) Isaac's heart started beating faster.

   (b) Isaac checked the room for evidence.

   (c) Uncle Pete threatened Isaac.

   (d) Isaac decided he had to get out of the cave.

3. Make a summary of Isaac's actions from after the front door slammed until he stomped his foot.

   - _____
   - _____
   - _____
   - _____
   - _____

4. Write a summary explaining Isaac's discoveries in the cave.

   _____

   _____

   _____

5. Make a summary listing what Isaac found in the wardrobe.

   _____

   _____

   _____

Name _____

> **Remember:**
> - The answers are usually not in the text, but there is information to give you clues to think about. (This could be underlined.)
> - Find the answer that makes the most sense and is supported by text details.
> - Always consider all possible answers before making a decision.

1. Most likely, how was Isaac feeling as he approached the stairs?

(a) afraid of being caught

(b) upset at being left home alone

(c) confused about his mysterious relatives

(d) anxious with anticipation

2. Why was Isaac sure the book he put in his pocket wouldn't be missed?

(a) It was covered in cardboard.

(b) There were five more similar books.

(c) The bookshelf was hidden by a cupboard.

(d) The bookshelf was full of books.

3. What is the best reason why Isaac gasped when he opened the wardrobe?

_____

_____

_____

4. Think about the things Isaac discovered and explain what you think Aunt Belinda and Uncle Pete were hiding.

_____

_____

_____

5. Uncle Pete tells Isaac, "Things are going to be very different."

(a) What do you think is going to be different? _____

_____

(b) Why did Uncle Pete need to do this? _____

_____

6. "I could easily escape past him, but I would have to be quick. I had to get away. It was my duty." Why do you think Isaac felt it was his duty to escape?

_____

_____

Lesson Objective

- Students will determine cause and effect and understand how they are connected.

Background Information

Students need to understand that a cause leads to an effect and that they are connected.

This section demonstrates strategies for students to use in order to find information in a text, which in turn helps them to make the connection and determine cause and effect.

They need to find and underline the keywords in questions, and then search for information in the text that makes connections between the keywords and either the cause or the effect. They need to understand that they will be given either a cause or an effect in the question, but they will need to search for the other.

Activity Answers

Easter Island ....**Pages 91–94**

- Practice Page: Page 93
    1. (b)
    2. They almost all died there from disease.
    3. They wanted to settle there because they could use the palms for boats and houses.
    4. (a)
    5. The war; kidnapping by slave traders; disease brought to the island by returning kidnap victims
- On Your Own: Page 94
    1. They would have fought each other to obtain food, as their own supplies were dwindling.
    2. (b)
    3. The trunks of the palm trees were used as rollers to transport the moai around the island.
    4. The Christian missionaries destroyed the moai along with some of the islanders sacred objects.
    5. The island had not previously known such diseases, and so the people were not immune to them.
    6. So many of the original islanders died.

Exercise Is Good for You ....**Pages 95–96**

- Try It Out: Page 96
    1. (d)
    2. The program would not be maintained as interest in the activity would be lost.
    3. Feeling of well-being, improved sleeping patterns, more toned body shape
    4. Answers will vary.
    5. An injury may occur.

Assessment Answers

Cause and Effect ....**Page 110**

    1. (a)
    2. (d)
    3. raw sensation in her throat; shaking; perspiration on forehead and neck
    4. She was ecstatic. She knew she would be auditioning for future productions.
    5. She changed from being shy and lacking in confidence to developing self-esteem and confidence in her ability.
    6. The familiar lines signaling her entry to the stage returned her confidence.

Lesson Objective

- Students will demonstrate their ability to identify facts and opinions and their understanding of how they differ.

Background Information

A fact is something that is true. It can be verified by referring to other information. In other words, it can be checked and be proven to be correct.

An opinion is something that someone believes to be true but cannot be verified. In other words, it is something that someone thinks rather than knows is true.

Students must be able to distinguish between facts and opinions in order to become critical readers. They have to engage and interact with text and read with a questioning attitude. They can then look for relationships and critically judge and evaluate what they read by identifying facts and opinions.

Critical readers become more discriminating consumers of the news media and advertising—an important life skill.

Activity Answers

The Beauty of Slovenia..**Pages 97–100**

- Practice Page: Page 99
  1. (a) fact   (b) opinion   (c) fact   (d) opinion
  2. Facts: Slovenia's capital city, old town, has parks, castle perched on summit of wooded hill, castle and museum give information about history of town and country.
     Opinions: charming town, buildings of great architectural interest, castle and museum are interesting places to visit.
  3. (a) The country has many physical features.   (b) blessed, outstanding, perfect destination
  4. Fact; Information can be verified to be true.
- On Your Own: Page 100
  1. (a) fact   (b) opinion   (c) opinion   (d) fact
  2. Gained independence in 1991; part of the former Yugoslavia; accepted into the UN in 1992; accepted into the European Union in 1994; has a castle, and the castle and museum provide information about the city's and country's history
  3. Triglav National Park is a true paradise; the beauty of the TNP captivates the hearts of all tourists; Skocjan Caves are awesome; the caves have many spectacular features; these leave visitors with an everlasting impression of the wonder and magnificence of nature; Secovlje saltpans are plain and unattractive; Cerknica Lake is an impressive phenomenon.
  4–6. Answers will vary.

Fabulous French Cuisine...**Pages 101–102**

- Try It Out: Page 102
  1. (c)   2. (a) opinion   (b) Answers will vary.
  3. Facts: same dish is not prepared/served in same way all over France; traditional recipes vary between provinces; regions of France use particular ingredients in their recipes; nouvelle cuisine became popular in the 1970s.
     Opinions: the beauty of French cooking comes from its distinctive provincial styles; great chefs of the world pride themselves in their ability to produce classic French recipes; cassoulet is a rich, wholesome stew; delicious food of France has something to please and delight everyone.
  4. Answers will vary.

Assessment Answers

Fact or Opinion..**Page 111**

  1. (d)
  2. Facts: Cerys and Emma were members of the youth theater group; Cerys had been chosen for a speaking role in the latest production; Cerys had never performed on stage before.
     Opinions: Amazingly, six months ago, she would have run the other way; her life had been transformed.
  3. (a) fact   (b) opinion   (c) opinion   (d) fact   (e) opinion
  4. (a) opinion   (b) It is what someone believes to be true.

Point of View and Purpose

Lesson Objective

- Students will understand and identify the writer's point of view and purpose.

Background Information

The writer's point of view is his or her opinion about a subject. A reader should, after careful and detailed analysis of what has been written, understand and be able to identify the point of view expressed in the text.

The writer's purpose for writing explains why the text was written. It may be to express a particular point of view, to amuse, entertain, inform, persuade, instruct, describe, record information, or to explain something.

Students should be encouraged to try to determine how and what the writer was thinking and use this to help them make decisions about the writer's point of view. They should then look for details in the text to support or reject the choices they have made. (These can be underlined.)

All possible choices should be considered before a final decision is made.

Activity Answers

Household Chores .... **Pages 103–106**

- Practice Page: Page 105
  1. (b)
  2. Sense of achievement; says thank you to parents; eases his mom's load; cares for his little sister; spends time with his family.
  3. They are foolish because they are not taking the opportunity to learn essential life skills.
  4. He enjoys it and believes it doesn't matter what you're doing as long as you're doing it together.
  5. Answers will vary.
- On Your Own: Page 106
  1. (d)
  2. (c)
  3. (a) learning important skills, communicating
     (b) learning gardening skills, communicating
     (c) alleviating his sister's stress with asthma
  4. Possible answers: It's important for everyone to help out; it helps relationships when everyone cooperates; you can learn from each other; you feel a part of a community.
  5. Answers will vary.

The Wind in the Willows .... **Pages 107–108**

- Try It Out: Page 108
  1. Possible answer: He appreciates it as an excellent piece of literature that has been used by so many in so many different ways.
  2. (d)
  3. Possible answer: to show that there are always many sides to a conflict or situation
  4. An adult—He used no illustrations, and the text was too difficult for a child to read and understand.
  5. Answers will vary.

Assessment Answers

Point of View and Purpose .... **Page 112**

  1. (b)
  2. (c)
  3. Possible answer: She probably would not have agreed, as she didn't even have the confidence to speak in front of a small group.
  4. Emma thought she was wonderful and hoped she was feeling okay.
  5. Answers will vary. Possible answers: proud of herself; believes in herself
  6. Answers will vary. Possible answer: to encourage young people to become involved in an activity that develops social skills

Helpful Hints

CAUSE AND EFFECT

- A cause (what happened first) leads to an effect (what happened as a result of the cause). They are connected.

- You are given either a cause or an effect, and you will need to find the other.

- Look for keywords in the question. Then, find the words in the text that are connected to the keywords.

- Check all possible answers before making a decision.

FACT OR OPINION

- A fact is something that can be checked and proven to be correct.

- An opinion is what someone believes to be true, but it can't be proven. Read the text to decide what can be proven (fact) by the text.

- Always check all possible answers before deciding on your answer.

POINT OF VIEW AND PURPOSE

- Writers do not always tell you what they believe. You may have to come to this conclusion based on the information you have read.

- Look for details and information in the text to help you decide why the author may have written the text or what the author's point of view is.

- Always check all possible answers before deciding on your answer.

Cause and Effect

Name _____

Cause and effect is a phrase we use to explain when one thing (a cause) makes something else happen (an effect). If you want to understand what you read, you must be able to determine the cause(s) and the effect(s) that take place in the text.

Activity: Read the passage below and complete pages 92–94.

Easter Island

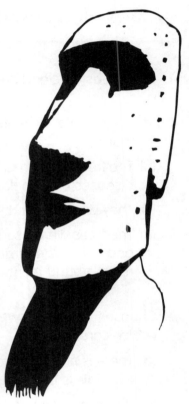

1. Easter Island (also known as "Rapa Nui") is an almost treeless island located in the South Pacific Ocean about 2,200 miles west of Chile. Around 63 square miles in area, it is one of the most isolated inhabited islands on Earth. But it is most famous for its 600 enormous, god-like statues that were constructed hundreds of years ago. About 15 of these have been restored to their original standing positions.

2. Scientists believe that Easter Island was first inhabited between CE (Common Era) 300 and 800. The settlers were most likely a group of Polynesian seafarers. At the time, the island would have been a welcome sight, as it was once covered in giant palms. The new inhabitants began to use the palms for building boats and houses.

3. By 1550, the population on the island was around 8,000. Evidence suggests that separate clans formed and were living in different areas of the island. All the clans seemed to be obsessed with a single goal—building statues called "moai." The moai were carved from the rock of one of the extinct volcanoes found on the island. Most of the moai are between 13 to 20 feet tall, but some are over 30 feet tall and weigh over 80 tons!

4. Many theories attempt to explain how the islanders constructed and moved the moai. It is known that they used hand picks to carve each statue from the rock, chipping away until the moai was held in place by a thin "keel." Some unfinished statues, which weigh almost 300 tons, are still in place. When a statue was finished, it was broken off the keel and moved using ropes tied to palm trunks. After some final decorations, the trunks were somehow used again as rollers to transport the moai across the island. The moai were then placed on prepared stone platforms. In some cases, the moai were moved along 12-mile tracks, a journey which must have taken a very long time.

5. The island clans competed to construct bigger statues. An unfortunate consequence of this was that they had to cut down a huge number of palm trees. In fact, sadly, one day someone chopped down the very last palm. The island's soil was eroding, and the islanders' crops failed. It seems that a violent war then broke out between the clans. Thousands of people died, and villages were destroyed. The moai were toppled and broken—by 1840, none were left standing.

6. When the violent war ended, the remaining islanders were in a terrible state. Little food was left, and no materials for making boats were available. Nonetheless, they still managed to rebuild their society and survive. In 1862, slave traders landed on the island. Around 1,500 islanders were kidnapped and taken to Peru. Almost all of these people died. A year later, the survivors returned to the island, but they now carried diseases like smallpox, causing even more deaths on Easter Island. Then, Christian missionaries arrived. In their efforts to convert the islanders to Christianity, many of the islanders' sacred objects were destroyed.

7. Today, over 5,000 people live on Easter Island. Most of these people are Polynesians and Chileans. There are some people who are related to the original Easter Islanders.

8. The tragic story of Easter Island is often described as a "story for our times." It is up to us to learn from the past.

Name _____

Follow the steps below to learn how you can determine the cause and effect.

- A cause leads to an effect, and they are connected.
- You will be told one, and you will need to identify the other.
- Look for keywords in the question and underline them.
- Find words in the text that are connected to the keywords.
- Always check all possible answers before making a decision.

1. Why is Easter Island an almost treeless island?

   (a) The climate prevents trees from growing there.

   (b) The trees were infected and died from diseases brought from Peru.

   (c) They were all used to make statues.

   (d) The trees were used for building boats and homes and transporting the huge moai around the island.

2. Choose the best answer. Think about each choice carefully.

   (a) There is nothing in the text to suggest this. This is not a good answer.

   (b) It was not the trees that were infected by diseases from outside the island. This is not a good answer.

   (c) Although the trees were required to transport the statues, they were not used to make them. This is not the best answer.

   (d) This explains exactly why the island is treeless. This is the best answer.

1. What caused the failure of the islanders' crops?

   (a) The crops were infected and died from diseases from Peru.

   (b) A volcano erupted and destroyed all the crops.

   (c) The crops could not grow because the soil was eroding.

   (d) The crops had no shade from the sun because the trees had all been used.

2. Choose the best answer. Think about each choice carefully.

   (a) It was not the crops that were affected by diseases from outside the island. This is not a good answer.

   (b) The text says nothing about active volcanoes. It refers only to the rock from extinct volcanoes used to carve the moai. This is not a good answer.

   (c) The soil was eroding. This is a very good answer, but you need to check all answers.

   (d) It is possible that the crops would have been adversely affected by the lack of shade, but this is not the reason given in the text. This is not the best answer.

Cause and Effect

Name _____

Use the strategies you learned to practice identifying cause and effect. Use the clues in the "Think!" boxes to help you.

1. What effect did the crop failure have on the island society?

   (a) The people left the island.

   (b) The clans engaged in a violent war in which thousands of people were killed.

   (c) The clans stole food from each other.

   (d) Many people died from starvation.

> **Think!**
> Read paragraph 5 carefully.

2. What was the effect of kidnapping about 1,500 islanders and taking them to Peru?

   _____

   _____

   _____

   _____

> **Think!**
> Read paragraph 6 to find the answer.

3. What effect did seeing the island covered with palms have on the Polynesian seafarers?

   _____

   _____

   _____

   _____

> **Think!**
> Read paragraph 2 and imagine what the sight meant to the seafarers.

4. After the war, why were the islanders no longer able to build boats?

   (a) There were no trees left from which to build the boats.

   (b) The people were too weak from lack of food.

   (c) They no longer had the tools for carving.

   (d) All the boatbuilders had been killed in the war.

> **Think!**
> What did they use to make boats?

5. Name the three events that had a huge impact on the island's population.

   • _____

   • _____

   • _____

> **Think!**
> Read paragraph 6 carefully.

Name _____

Use the strategies you have been practicing to help you identify cause and effect.

1. Most likely, why did the islanders resort to violence after the failure of the crops?

_____

_____

_____

2. By 1840, none of the moai were left standing. Why was this?

(a) They were blown over in the wind.

(b) During the war, clans toppled the moai of rival clans.

(c) They had been destroyed by the Christian missionaries.

(d) The were knocked down by the force of earth tremors.

3. If moai were carved from rock, explain why so many palm trees were required.

_____

_____

_____

4. What effect did the arrival of the Christian missionaries have on the state of the moai?

_____

_____

_____

5. The survivors of the slave trade who had returned home to Easter Island had been exposed to many diseases. Explain why this would have had such a devastating effect on the island's population.

_____

_____

_____

6. Why are there few people related to the original islanders left on Easter Island?

_____

_____

_____

Cause and Effect

Name _____

Activity: Read the passage below and complete page 96.

Exercise Is Good for You

1. Exercise is good for you, but do you know why?

2. Exercise has a positive effect on the whole body, including the mind. During exercise, chemicals called *endorphins* are released, which create a feeling of happiness and well-being. This in turn improves self-esteem, confidence, and overall body image. Exercise also increases energy levels and improves sleeping patterns.

3. Exercise also produces a visible improvement in the body. Because exercise burns calories as fuel and develops muscles, the body shape looks better and more toned. Excess calories consumed will not be stored as fat if they are used as fuel for exercise.

4. Keeping a healthy, stable weight can also prevent the development of some diseases, particularly type II diabetes, which is becoming more common in younger people. Weight-bearing exercises, such as running and walking, help to strengthen the bones and prevent bone weakness in later life.

5. It is recommended that everyone should do at least 30 minutes of exercise every day. When planning an exercise routine, it is important to choose enjoyable activities, otherwise it will be difficult to maintain motivation. There are three parts to a well-balanced exercise plan: aerobic exercise, strength development, and flexibility training.

6. Aerobic exercise develops the heart and increases the lungs' capacity for taking in and using oxygen. The cardiovascular system, the heart, and blood vessels work more efficiently distributing oxygen around the body. Activities such as swimming, running, cycling, and dancing can provide an excellent aerobic workout, but they must be performed at a level that requires you to breathe more rapidly.

7. Strength-development activities provide specific workouts for particular muscle groups, such as cycling and running for leg muscles and swimming for the arms and upper body. As the muscles develop, they allow exercise to be maintained for longer periods before getting tired, and they help to protect the body from strain and injury during exercise. Muscle is more efficient than fat at burning calories, so the more muscle you have, the more effective your body is at burning fuel.

8. Exercise helps to maintain the body's flexibility, allowing the muscles and joints to move freely. This improves performance as the body moves more easily and efficiently. A flexible body is less prone to injury, strains, and sprains than a stiff body. Performing simple stretching exercises during activity improves flexibility. To prevent injury, stretching exercises should only be done after the body has warmed up.

9. Just as an engine requires fuel to work, the body requires fuel in the form of calories, which we get from food. To maintain a healthy weight, it is necessary to consume sufficient calories to allow the body to exercise and function normally. Sometimes, an engine malfunctions and needs time off in the workshop to be repaired. Our bodies also malfunction at times, giving in to injuries and infections. When this occurs, it is essential to rest and recuperate. When exercise is resumed, it is done gradually, increasing the effort as the body regains its strength.

10. Exercise is good for you! Now you know why.

Name _____

Use the strategies you learned and practiced in *Easter Island* to help you identify cause and effect.

> ## Remember:
> * A cause leads to an effect, and they are connected.
> * You will be told one, and you will need to identify the other.
> * Look for keywords in the question and underline them.
> * Find words in the text that are connected to the keywords in the question.
> * Always check all possible answers before making a decision.

1. What effect does exercise have on the brain?

   (a) It makes you so tired you feel confused.

   (b) It prevents you from sleeping.

   (c) It produces endorphins, which make you sleep better.

   (d) It produces endorphins, which make you feel happy.

   | **Think!** |
   | Read paragraph 2 carefully. |

2. What would be the effect of choosing an exercise program of activities you did not enjoy?

   _____

   _____

   _____

3. List some of the obvious effects of an exercise program.

   _____

   _____

   _____

   _____

4. Name some activities that you do or could participate in to improve your health.

   _____

   _____

   _____

5. What would be the effect of performing stretching exercises before the body is warmed up?

   _____

   _____

   _____

Fact or Opinion

Name _____

When reading, it is important to understand the difference between facts and opinions and to be able to distinguish which is which. A fact is something that is true. An opinion is something that someone *believes* is true.

Activity: Read the passage below and complete pages 98–100.

The Beauty of Slovenia

1. Nestled in the heart of Europe, bordering Italy, Austria, Hungary, Croatia, and a short stretch of the Adriatic Sea, lies the small country of Slovenia. Prior to its independence in 1991, the Republic of Slovenia was a part of the former Yugoslavia, which experienced many turbulent years at the end of the millennium. In May 1992, Slovenia was accepted into the United Nations and two years later, into the European Union. The way was then clear for the small country to develop as a democratic nation.

2. Slovenia has continued to improve its economy since independence, particularly in the tourist industry. Each year, more than a million visitors from other European countries vacation in Slovenia, and new resorts are being built to meet the demands of the booming industry. The climate guarantees warm summers and plenty of snow in the winter.

3. The country is blessed with many outstanding physical features that make it the perfect destination for a vacation—mountains, lakes, rivers, forests, and natural and thermal springs. Areas of primeval forest can still be found; the largest of which is in the Kocevje region in the south of the country, where a chance encounter with a brown bear is still possible.

4. A number of regions within Slovenia are of international environmental significance:

    *   In the far northwest lies the remarkable Triglav National Park, a true paradise of majestic mountains, valleys, lakes, and waterfalls. The park, named Triglav (meaning "three heads") after Slovenia's highest peak, has a diverse plant and animal population. The beauty of this region captivates the hearts of all those who visit.

    *   Situated close to Ljubljana, the country's capital, are the awesome Skocjan Caves—a network of eleven caves with a number of spectacular features, such as the swallow holes and natural bridges, which leave the visitor with an everlasting impression of the wonder and magnificence of nature.

    *   Although an unattractive and plain sight to behold, the very special ecological conditions that have been created in the coastal Secovlje saltpans have seen many of Slovenia's endangered plant species flourish. About 80 species of birds nest there regularly.

    *   Cerknica Lake, to the southwest of Ljubljana, is an impressive phenomenon. When full to capacity, it is the largest lake in the country, but during the dry season, it can be completely emptied as the water drains through underground streams. With the autumn rains and the snows melting in the spring, the underground streams swell. The level of the lake then rises, and the volume of water can no longer be contained.

5. Slovenia's capital city, Ljubljana, is a charming old town with many parks and buildings of great architectural interest. Perched on the summit of a wooded hill, Ljubljana Castle dominates the capital. Along with the National Museum, the castle is a very interesting place to visit, providing insight into the history of this wonderful old town and country.

Fact or Opinion

Name _____

Follow the steps below to learn how you can determine if something is a fact or an opinion.

- Ask yourself:

  Can the statement be checked and proven to be correct? If it can, it is a fact.

  Is it what someone *thinks* is true and can't be proven? If so, it is an opinion.

  > For example: Hens lay eggs. (Fact)
  >
  > Eggs taste good. (Opinion)

- Always check all possible answers before making a decision.

1. Which sentence states a fact?

  (a) People love the old charm of Ljubljana.

  (b) Slovenia is better now that it is an independent nation.

  (c) Tourists love the physical beauty of Slovenia.

  (d) Slovenia is a European country.

2. Choose the best answer. Think about each choice carefully.

  (a) Not all people may agree with this statement, and there is no way of checking how people feel. This is an opinion.

  (b) For some people this may be correct, but others may disagree. This is an opinion.

  (c) Not all people may appreciate Slovenia's scenery. This is an opinion.

  (d) This is a fact that can be verified in atlases and in documentation that covers the political status of all nations. This is the only possible answer.

1. Which sentence contains two facts?

  (a) Ljubljana is the capital city of Slovenia.

  (b) Cerknica Lake, to the southwest of Ljubljana, is an impressive phenomenon.

  (c) Areas of primeval forest can still be found in Slovenia, the largest of which is in the Kocevje region.

  (d) Slovenia has many areas of beauty that make it a perfect vacation destination.

2. Choose the best answer. Think about each choice carefully.

  (a) This is only one fact that can be verified. You need two facts. This is not a good answer.

  (b) This sentence contains one fact and one opinion. The position of the lake can be verified, so it is a fact. Whether it is an impressive phenomenon is dependent on individual opinion. This is not the best answer.

  (c) This sentence contains two statements that can be verified: areas of primeval forest can still be found in Slovenia, and the largest area of primeval forest is in the Kocevje region. This is a very good answer, but check all of them.

  (d) This sentence contains two opinions. Maybe not everyone would agree that Slovenia is a beautiful country, and people's ideas of a perfect vacation vary greatly. This is not a good answer.

Fact or Opinion

Name _____

Use the strategies you learned to practice identifying facts and opinions. Use the clues in the "Think!" boxes to help you.

1. Mark the correct box.

	Fact	Opinion
(a) Slovenia is a country in Europe.	☐	☐
(b) The Slovenes are happy to be in the European Union.	☐	☐
(c) Slovenia gained independence in 1991.	☐	☐
(d) The climate of Slovenia is wonderful.	☐	☐

> **Think!**
> Which statements can be verified conclusively?

2. Write three facts and three opinions about Ljubljana.

Facts	Opinions

> **Think!**
> Read the final paragraph carefully.

3. Read this sentence from the text.

> *The country is blessed with many outstanding physical features that make it the perfect destination for a vacation.*

(a) Rewrite the sentence giving its factual information only.

_____

_____

(b) List the key "opinion" words from the original sentence.

_____

_____

> **Think!**
> Opinions often include adjectives and descriptive verbs.

4. Read this sentence from the text.

> *The park, named Triglav (meaning "three heads") after Slovenia's highest peak, has a diverse plant and animal population.*

This sentence is . . . ☐ a fact. ☐ an opinion.

Explain your answer.

_____

_____

> **Think!**
> Facts can be conclusively verified.

Name _____

Use the strategies you have been practicing to help you distinguish between facts and opinions.

1. Mark the correct box.

	Fact	Opinion
(a) Slovenia joined the United Nations in 1992.	☐	☐
(b) Other Europeans vacation in Slovenia because it is cheap.	☐	☐
(c) The physical beauty of Slovenia is its main attraction.	☐	☐
(d) Brown bears can be found in the south of the country.	☐	☐

2. Write five facts about Slovenia's history and its capital city, Ljubljana.

- _____
- _____
- _____
- _____
- _____

3. Write five opinions from the passage about the physical features of Slovenia.

- _____
- _____
- _____
- _____
- _____

4. Write four key facts from paragraph 2.

- _____
- _____
- _____
- _____

5. Write three words or phrases the author uses to describe Slovenia.

- _____
- _____
- _____

6. What do you believe is the author's opinion of Slovenia?

_____

_____

Fact or Opinion

Name _____

Activity: Read the passage below and complete page 102.

Fabulous French Cuisine

1. France is famous for many things: the Tour de France, the Eiffel Tower, the French Revolution, but most importantly, French cuisine. Not many people realize that it is the Italians we have to thank for the fabulous food of France! In the 16th century, Italian noblewoman Catherine de Medici married the French king, Henri II. She was so disgusted by the cooking methods of the French aristocracy that she decided to bring high-quality chefs from Italy to teach those of the French court how to enhance the flavor and quality of ingredients. And so French cuisine was born, becoming the standard by which all other Western cuisines are measured.

2. For the French people, enjoying food is a part of their culture. On weekends and at holiday times, dinner can be a long, drawn-out affair involving a number of courses. They take great pride in the preparation and presentation of their dishes and strive to use the freshest and best of ingredients. All French towns have fresh produce markets, which are always well patronized by visitors to the area as well as the locals. Choosing locally produced foods is important to the French people and is responsible for the continued interest in local specialties.

3. Great chefs of the world pride themselves in their ability to produce classic French recipes to a very high standard of excellence—*haute cuisine* (meaning "high cooking"). The beauty of French cooking comes from its distinctive provincial styles, so a person traveling around France will notice that the same dish is not prepared and served in the same way in different parts of the country because traditional recipes vary between provinces. For example, *cassoulet*, a rich, wholesome stew made with various meats, vegetables, beans, oils, and aromatic herbs is made throughout France, yet there are many variations. Followers of each recipe claim theirs to be the original!

4. The regions of France are also well known for using particular ingredients in their recipes:
    - Butter, cream, and apples are widely featured in recipes from the northwest.
    - Duck fat, *foie gras* (made from goose liver), porcini mushrooms, and gizzards are commonly prepared in the southwest.
    - Typically, the southeast (Mediterranean) uses olive oil, herbs, and tomatoes extensively in its recipes.
    - The recipes of eastern France reflect the region's proximity to Germany, with lard, sausages, and sauerkraut regularly appearing on the menu.
    - Potatoes, pork, and endives are commonly served in northern France.

5. Famous French dishes include souffle, crepes, *coq au vin* (chicken cooked in red wine), *canard au sang* (pressed duck), steak *au poivre* (peppered steak), and *cassoulet*. Frog legs and *escargots* (snails) are rarely eaten in France, despite their fame.

6. Nouvelle cuisine became popular in the 1970s and offers a lighter alternative to the traditional recipes. The emphasis of nouvelle cuisine is on small portions, lightly cooked vegetables, and fruit-based sauces. The same care and attention to detail is given to the preparation of these new recipes, which offer a healthier alternative to the traditional dishes.

7. Whatever your preference, the delicious food of France has something to please and delight everyone. The only possible problem is one of too much choice!

Name _____

Use the strategies you learned and practiced in *The Beauty of Slovenia* to help you distinguish between facts and opinions.

> **Remember:**
> - Ask yourself:
>   Can the statement be checked and proven to be correct? If it can, it is a fact.
>   Is it what someone *thinks* is true and can't be proven? If so, it is an opinion.
> - Always check all possible answers before making a decision.

1. Which sentence states an opinion?

(a) France is famous for many things.

(b) Food is part of the French culture.

(c) The beauty of French cooking comes from its distinctive provincial styles.

(d) Traditional recipes vary between provinces.

2. Read the sentence from the text.

Choosing locally produced foods is important to the French people and is responsible for the continued interest in local specialties.

(a) This statement is . . . ☐ a fact. ☐ an opinion.

(b) Explain your answer.

_____

_____

_____

3. Write two facts and two opinions given by the author about French cuisine.

Facts	Opinions

4. What do you believe is the author's opinion of French food? Explain your answer.

_____

_____

_____

_____

Point of View and Purpose

Name _____

When we read, we should try to think like the writer to figure out how and what he or she feels and believes about the subject (point of view) and why he or she wrote the text (purpose).

Activity: Read the story below and complete pages 104–106.

Household Chores

1. Some people think that looking after a house is the responsibility of the adults who live there, not the children. I disagree. I think everyone should be given responsibilities appropriate to their age and ability.

2. I really enjoy doing household chores. Although I'm only 13 years old, I understand that the things Mom and Dad teach me at home now will stay with me forever and help me when I have a house of my own to look after. I get a real sense of achievement when I complete a chore and someone says to me, "Great job, Tom."

3. My friends think I'm crazy. They ask me why I waste my time with housework when there's someone else to do it. I always answer the same thing: There are so many different skills involved in housework; why waste the opportunity to learn something new? Besides, the more stuff I can do, the more I can help Mom and Dad. They do so much for me, so it's my way of saying, "Thank you."

4. My friends laugh because I help with the ironing. They say ironing is just a waste of time, but I disagree. I don't like to wear clothes that haven't been ironed, so I think I should take some responsibility for ironing them. It's quite a tricky business getting the folds just right and ironing in the creases. I understand now why it's not Mom's favorite chore; the pile never seems to get smaller! I'm glad I'm able to help.

5. Attacking a room with a feather duster is actually great fun. I start with the light fixtures and work my way down to the baseboards, then I do the window blinds. It's amazing how much dust settles in a week! Friends think it doesn't matter if the house is dusty, but my little sister has asthma, and I know how she would suffer if we didn't clean the house regularly.

6. My dad is a really good handyman, and he's taught me lots of DIY ("do-it-yourself") projects. I'm not strong enough yet to do some of the jobs, but at least I know how to do them. You can save a lot of money if you can do a job yourself instead of always having to hire someone, and you don't have to wait around for them to show up! My friends say they'd rather be playing games with their dads. I enjoy that, too, but I think any time spent with my dad is great, whatever we're doing.

7. Mom is a really great gardener. She's always out in the yard with her gloves on. She's taught me how to grow and look after different types of plants. Our garden always looks amazing. I'll have one of my own one day. I'd love to be able to design it from scratch. My friends don't take any notice of their gardens and wouldn't recognize a weed if it attacked them. I think a tidy yard is really important. If all the residents in the street keep their yards tidy, the whole area looks so much nicer.

8. In the kitchen, my dad is a real chef. He loves experimenting with different ingredients, and he tries recipes from all over the world. He calls me his apprentice chef, and together we concoct the most delicious meals. When I have my own house, I won't have to worry about eating frozen meals like my friends will. They love coming for dinner at our house but never offer to help with the preparation or clearing up. They wouldn't know how.

9. I can't imagine living at home and not helping out. We spend a lot of time together, sharing everything and learning from one another. Even my little sister keeps her bedroom and toys tidy. I'll always help out in the house, wherever I'm living. My friends may be laughing at me now, but in the end, I think I'll have the last laugh!

Name _____

Follow the steps below to learn how to identify the writer's point of view and his or her probable purpose for writing the text.

- Writers don't always just tell you what they think or believe or why they have written the text. Sometimes, you have to try to think like they do and form a conclusion based on the information you have read.
- In the text, there are details and information related to the question for you to find, underline, and use in making your choices.
- Always consider all possible answers before making a decision.

1. The writer believes that:

(a) children should be allowed to play instead of work in the home.

(b) working in the home is not safe for children.

(c) children should choose whether or not they work in the home.

(d) all children should be given jobs they are capable of doing.

2. Choose the best answer. Think about each choice carefully.

(a) The writer mentions nothing about children playing. This is not a good answer.

(b) The writer does not discuss the safety aspect of children working in the home. This is not a good answer.

(c) The writer may agree with this, but he thinks everyone should have responsibilities. This is not the best answer.

(d) This statement covers the writer's opinion on children working at home. This is the best answer.

1. Most likely, what is the writer's probable purpose for writing the text?

(a) He wants to explain to his teacher why he didn't have time to do his homework over the weekend.

(b) He wants the reader to know what a great boy he is.

(c) He wants his mom and dad to realize just how much he does around the house.

(d) He wants to share all the positive things he has learned and achieved through helping with the chores at home.

2. Choose the best answer. Think about each choice carefully.

(a) The writer is talking about how he helps at home all the time, not just during one weekend. This is not a good answer.

(b) The writer includes the things he gains from the work, not just how helpful he is to others. This is not a good answer.

(c) This would imply that his parents complain that he doesn't do enough. The text suggests that his relationships with all his family are very positive. This is not the best answer.

(d) Every paragraph gives an example of the writer's positive achievements and experiences through helping at home. This is the best answer.

Point of View and Purpose

Name _____

Use the strategies you learned to practice identifying what the writer believes about the subject and why he or she wrote the text. Use the clues in the "Think!" boxes to help you.

1. Why does the writer think it is important for children to learn how to do household chores?

   (a) The house will be very dirty if they don't help.

   (b) Children who help will learn how to look after a house when they're older.

   (c) Children who help will feel a sense of achievement.

   (d) It's important to say "thank you" to your parents.

   Think! Underline the keywords in the question.

2. Write three personal reasons why the writer likes to do household chores.

   • _____

   • _____

   • _____

   Think! How do his efforts help him, not the house?

3. How does the writer feel about his friends' attitude toward household chores?

   _____
   _____
   _____

   Think! Reread the paragraphs in which his friends are mentioned.

4. Explain how the writer feels about spending his time with his family.

   _____
   _____
   _____

   Think! Paragraph 6 gives you the strongest clue.

5. What is your point of view about children helping with household chores?

   _____
   _____
   _____
   _____
   _____

   Think! How much do you help at home? How much more or less would your family like you to do?
   Do you think your parents' demands are reasonable or unreasonable?

Name _____

Use the strategies you have been practicing to help you identify the writer's point of view and purpose.

1. What do the writer's friends think about him doing household chores?
   (a) They don't know that he does any domestic chores.
   (b) They don't care enough to have an opinion.
   (c) They say he's crazy but secretly wish they were doing the same thing.
   (d) They think he's foolish for doing chores when he could be doing his "own thing" instead.

2. How does the writer feel about his friends' comments about housework?
   (a) They make him feel very upset.
   (b) They show that his friends are very selfish.
   (c) He thinks his friends are rather foolish and should try to do some work around the house.
   (d) When they are all older, his friends will realize that he had been right to learn how to do the work.

3. The writer feels that the time spent with his family is more important than the activity. What positive outcomes in his relationship with his family could he gain by . . .
   (a) doing DIY projects with his father? _____

   _____

   (b) gardening with his mother? _____

   _____

   (c) dusting the house? _____

   _____

4. What are the key points the writer is trying to get across to his audience?

   _____

   _____

   _____

   _____

   _____

   _____

5. Has the writer influenced your thoughts on children helping at home? ☐ Yes ☐ No
   Explain your answer.

   _____

   _____

Name _____

Activity: Read the passage below and complete page 108.

The Wind in the Willows

1. One of the 20th century's great works of literature was *The Wind in the Willows* by the Scottish author Kenneth Grahame. He completed this, his fourth and final book, in 1908. In true classic style, the book has been enjoyed by millions of readers worldwide and has been the catalyst for other works of literature.

2. Like two of his earlier books, the original text indicates that *The Wind in the Willows* was penned for adults, yet the characters and their adventures suggest that the story would also have widespread appeal to children of all ages. In its original state, the story would have been available only to those children who had someone who could change the text to an easier level. Illustrations for the text were added in 1931 when E.H. Shepherd, illustrator for the *Winnie the Pooh* classics, sketched the characters and scenes in his famous style. Now many different adaptations of this classic are in print, suitable for all ages.

3. At one level, the story relates the adventures of Ratty, Mole, and Toad as they enjoy their lives on the riverbank, meeting up with their friends, Badger, Otter, and his son, Portly. Ratty, Mole, and Badger fight a constant battle to keep the extravagant Toad out of mischief and trouble. It tells also of their encounters with the creatures of the Wild Wood, the stoats and weasels, and rabbits and squirrels.

4. At a higher level, the story describes the social strata of British society in the early 20th century, each character portraying a role within the class structure; the riverbank inhabitants representing the upper class and the Wild Wood creatures representing the working class. The events of the story correspond to typical situations as they could have occurred in Britain at that time.

5. A.A. Milne, author of the classic *Winnie the Pooh* stories, adapted *The Wind in the Willows* for the stage. He concentrated mainly on the escapades of Toad, as these were more easily adjusted to fit a stage production. He called the play *Toad of Toad Hall*. It had its first showing in London in December 1929, and like Grahame's book, *Toad of Toad Hall* has become a classic masterpiece, and it has been staged many times throughout the 20th century and into the 21st.

6. There have also been many versions of *The Wind in the Willows* for film and television. The most faithful being the 1983 Cosgrove Hall animated film version, which was followed with a television series by the same company.

7. Although Kenneth Grahame died before E.H. Shepherd's illustrations for his book were complete, more tales from the riverbank have continued to delight us, as the author William Horwood has written a number of sequels to *The Wind in the Willows*:

   - *The Willows in Winter*, 1995
   - *Toad Triumphant*, 1996
   - *The Willows and Beyond*, 1997
   - *The Willows at Christmas*, 2001

8. In 1981, *Wild Wood* by Jan Needle was published, retelling the story of *The Wind in the Willows* from the point of view of the Wild Wood inhabitants. Although written many years after the original, *Wild Wood* also delivers a story of social history, describing the dramatic changes to British society with the election of the first female prime minister in 1979.

9. One hundred years later, the classic tale of *The Wind in the Willows* is still stirring the hearts and minds of book lovers everywhere.

Name _____

Use the strategies you learned and practiced in *Household Chores* to help you identify the writer's point of view and purpose.

> **Remember:**
> - Writers don't always just tell you what they think or believe or why they have written the text. Sometimes, you have to try to think like they do and form a conclusion based on what you've read.
> - In the text, there are details and information related to the question for you to find and use in making your choices. (These could be underlined.)
> - Always consider all possible answers before making a decision.

1. What do you believe is the writer's opinion of *The Wind in the Willows*?

_____

_____

2. What was the writer's purpose in writing this piece of text?

(a) He enjoys books with animal characters.

(b) He wanted everyone to know how much he loved the book.

(c) He wanted to explain how the book could appeal to adults and children.

(d) He wanted to explain how the story had developed into a masterpiece, appreciated all over the world.

3. Why do you think Jan Needle chose to write *Wild Wood*?

_____

_____

_____

4. When Kenneth Grahame wrote *The Wind in the Willows*, was he most likely writing for an adult or child audience? Explain your answer.

_____

_____

5. Complete the information about a story you have read with animal characters that was written with the purpose of teaching lessons about life.

Title: _____

Author (and Illustrator): _____

_____

Characters: _____

_____

Lesson(s): _____

_____

Name _____

Activity: Read the story below, and use pages 110–112 to show how well you can identify cause and effect, fact or opinion, and point of view and purpose.

Stage Fright

1. "Oh, Cerys, you look fabulous!" cried Emma as her best friend waltzed into the room, showing off the first of her stage costumes. "I'm so excited for you."

2. "Me, too, sweetie," squealed Cerys as she leaned forward to kiss the air on each side of Emma's head. "Well, tonight's the night! Let the world see a future Oscar winner!"

3. The two girls were members of the local youth theater group, and Cerys had been chosen for a speaking role in the latest production. She had never performed on stage before, and even more amazingly, six months ago, would have run the other way if anyone had suggested speaking in front of even a small group. Ever since reading the flyer, her life had been transformed.

ATTENTION
ALL 11-15-YEAR-OLDS
Looking for something new
and challenging?
**Give
Newtown Youth Theater Group
a try!**

• Meet new friends
• Boost your confidence
• Improve your communication skills
• Develop positive body language
• Have lots of fun!

Contact Angela (222) 123-4555

4. At the theater, there was an atmosphere of great excitement with greetings from fellow actors and best wishes from friends and families. Last-minute jobs were hurriedly being attended to by the stagehands, and makeup artists were adding final touches to the actors' faces. Cerys enjoyed being a part of the excitement in the dressing room, and it wasn't until she was waiting in the wings for her first cue that she felt a raw sensation in her throat. She began to feel very strange. She couldn't stop shaking and beads of perspiration dampened her forehead and the back of her neck. In her mind, she saw a sea of faces laughing at her as she struggled to remember her lines and stage positions.

5. "I can't do it. I can't go on!" she hissed to George, the prompter, who was standing beside her with his clipboard. "I can't do it. I just can't."

6. She turned to run, but as she did so, she heard the familiar lines signaling her entry onto the stage. She stopped suddenly, turned to George, and mouthed, "I'm on, George. I'm on right now!" The wooden floorboards creaked as she strode on to center stage and delivered her well rehearsed lines.

7. During intermission, Emma embraced her friend. "Oh, Cerys, you were magnificent! George told me what happened. Was it nerves? Are you okay now?"

8. "Okay? You're asking me if I'm okay?" Cerys was ecstatic. "Emma, I thought I'd be able to see all the faces, but it was all black out there. I just focused on the center of the blackness, and I was fine! It was fantastic. I felt such a buzz. I can't wait to get on again!"

9. For the rest of the evening, Cerys was in a trance. Each time she walked on stage, she felt as though she owned it, speaking her lines as naturally as if they were her own. As the curtain fell after the final scene, Cerys knew she would be auditioning for the next production, and the one after that . . .

10. Preparing for bed that night, the sound of applause still ringing in her ears, Cerys thought of how much she had changed since joining the youth theater such a short time ago. From her bedside table she took out a well-worn piece of paper. Reading it again, she thought, "Well, it certainly worked for me!"

Name _____

> ## Remember:
> - A cause leads to an effect, and they are connected.
> - You will be told one, and you will need to identify the other.
> - Look for keywords in the question and underline them.
> - Find words in the text that are connected to the keywords.
> - Check all possible answers before making a decision.

1. Why were Cerys and Emma so excited?

   (a) Cerys was performing in a play at the theater.

   (b) Cerys was showing off new clothes.

   (c) They were going to the theater.

   (d) They were trying on new costumes.

2. Why did Cerys feel strange while waiting in the wings?

   (a) She was feeling ill.

   (b) She had forgotten all her lines.

   (c) The audience was laughing at her.

   (d) She had an attack of stage fright.

3. What effect did stage fright have on Cerys?

   _____

   _____

   _____

4. How did Cerys feel after the production finished?

   _____

   _____

   _____

5. Most likely, how had being part of the youth theater group changed Cerys?

   _____

   _____

   _____

6. What caused Cerys to change her mind about running away and not performing?

   _____

   _____

   _____

Fact or Opinion

Assessment

Name _____

> **Remember:**
> - A fact can be checked and proven to be correct.
> - An opinion is what someone *believes* to be true, but it can't be proven.
> - Always check all possible answers before making a decision.

1. Which sentence states a fact?

   (a) The play was a resounding success.

   (b) The audience was well entertained.

   (c) The makeup and scenery looked very professional.

   (d) Cerys overcame her stage fright.

2. Write three facts and two opinions from the third paragraph.

   Facts:

   - _____

   - _____

   - _____

   Opinions:

   - _____

   - _____

3. Mark the correct box.   Fact   Opinion

   (a) People greeted each other at the theater.   ☐   ☐

   (b) Everyone enjoyed the excitement.   ☐   ☐

   (c) The atmosphere at the theater was exciting.   ☐   ☐

   (d) Stagehands completed last-minute jobs.   ☐   ☐

   (e) The actors were too nervous before the show.   ☐   ☐

4. *Let the world see a future Oscar winner!*

   (a) Is the statement above a fact or an opinion?   ☐ Fact   ☐ Opinion

   (b) Explain your answer. _____

   _____

   _____

   _____

Name _____

> **Remember:**
> - Writers don't always tell you what they believe, so you may have to form a conclusion based on what you've read.
> - There are details and information you can find, underline, and use to help you to do this.
> - Always consider all possible answers before making a decision.

1. Most likely, what is the best reason why Cerys joined the theater group?

    (a) She had nothing better to do.

    (b) She needed to boost her confidence and improve her social skills.

    (c) She wanted to make more friends because Emma was her only friend.

    (d) Her friend Emma suggested it.

2. How did Cerys feel at the end of the performance?

    (a) She couldn't wait to leave the stage.

    (b) She was glad the first night was over.

    (c) She had enjoyed herself so much, she wanted to perform in more plays.

    (d) She felt happy and relieved.

3. What would Cerys have thought about performing in a play a few months prior?

_____

_____

_____

4. Explain what Emma thought about Cerys during intermission.

_____

_____

_____

5. Explain what you think Cerys' point of view of herself is now after being a member of the youth theater and performing.

_____

_____

_____

6. What do you think is the writer's purpose in writing this text?

_____

_____

_____